Carey Jewitt • Sara Price
Kerstin Leder Mackley • Nikoleta Yiannoutsou
Douglas Atkinson

Interdisciplinary Insights for Digital Touch Communication

Carey Jewitt
UCL Knowledge Lab, Institute of Education
University College London
London, UK

Sara Price
UCL Knowledge Lab, Institute of Education
University College London
London, UK

Kerstin Leder Mackley
UCL Knowledge Lab, Institute of Education
University College London
London, UK

Nikoleta Yiannoutsou
UCL Knowledge Lab, Institute of Education
University College London
London, UK

Douglas Atkinson
UCL Knowledge Lab, Institute of Education
University College London
London, UK

https://doi.org/10.1007/978-3-030-24564-1

This book is dedicated to Gunther Kress (1940–2019).

Acknowledgements

The research reported in this book is undertaken as a part of the InTouch project, a European Research Council Consolidator Award (Award Number: 681489).

The authors would like to thank the following people and organizations, especially those people who participated in the InTouch case study research:

Caroline Yan Zhang (Royal College of Art, UK) and Romain Meunier (UCL Institute of Making) for their facilitation of the rapid prototyping sessions as part of the Imagining Remote Personal Touch case study.

Dr. Emma Zhang and Professor Adrian Cheok for the loan of a pair of Kissenger devices used within the Imagining Remote Personal Touch case study.

The members of the Invisible Flock Artist Studio, who are collaborators on the Art of Remote Contact case study. The Remote Contact Exhibition was supported by FACT and Community Integrated Care, funded by Arts Council England and Leeds City Council, with the support of a Wellcome Trust Arts Award, in collaboration with Prof. Nadia Berthouze (UCL).

Owlet Baby Care, specifically Dr. Milena Adamian and Michelle Dangerfield, for the loan of four smart sock units to support the InTouch with Baby case study.

Dr. Aikaterini Fotopoulou, Professor Nadia Berthouze and Frederik Brudy, who are collaborators on the Tactile Emoticon case study, and the UCL Social Science Plus scheme, who provided additional funding for this collaboration.

Dr. Val Mitchell and Dr. Garrath T. Wilson, Loughborough University School of Design and Creative Arts, who are collaborators on the Designing Digital Touch case study.

Evy Samuelsson, InTouch Project administrator.

Lili Golmohammadi, a Doctoral Student on InTouch, particularly for her contribution to the development and design of the Designing Digital Touch Toolkit.

Contents

About the Authors

Douglas Atkinson is a Research Fellow at London College of Fashion, University of the Arts London, and guest lectures on fashion and digital technologies at a number of universities. His research interests include touch perception of physical and digital objects and the sensory and emotional experience of making, particularly in the context of off-shored production, materially detached from the designer. He is currently undertaking a PhD on the role of touch in the hands-on development of a garment, within the InTouch project. He was Research Associate on the 'Digital Sensoria: Design Through Digital Perceptual Experience' project and Co-investigator on the MIDAS 'Methodological Innovation in Digital Arts and Social Sciences' project.

Carey Jewitt is Professor of Learning and Technology at UCL Knowledge Lab, University College London, and is currently Director of InTouch (funded by an ERC Consolidator Award). Her research interests include multimodal research theory and methods and methodological innovation, bringing this social perspective to touch and technology-mediated interaction more generally. She has led numerous research projects in these areas and previously led the large NCRM-funded project MODE 'Multimodal Methods for Researching Digital Data and Environments' (MODE.ioe.ac.uk). She is the Founding Editor of the journal *Visual Communication* (Sage) and has published extensively in her fields. Her most recent books include *Introducing Multimodality* (2016) and *The Routledge Handbook of Multimodal Analysis* (2014).

Kerstin Leder Mackley is a Senior Research Fellow on InTouch at the UCL Knowledge Lab, University College London. Her research interests are in sensory and visual ethnographic research approaches as applied to the study of everyday experiences and activities, emerging technologies and design futures. She has been a Research Fellow on a number of significant projects, including 'LEEDR: Low Effort Energy Demand Reduction' (Loughborough Uni.) and 'TOTeM: Tales of Things and electronic Memory' (Brunel Uni.). Her recent publications include *Making Homes: Ethnography and Design* (2017) with Pink, Moroşanu, Mitchell and Bhamra. She has published in a range of journals, notably in *Qualitative Research*, *Media, Culture & Society* and *Visual Studies*.

Sara Price is Professor of Digital Learning at UCL Knowledge Lab and Co-I on InTouch. Her research interests focus on the design, development and evaluation of emerging digital technologies for learning, teaching and training with attention to embodiment, how sensory and bodily interaction can be mediated through digital technology and the role of this in supporting new ways of thinking and meaning-making. She is UCL PI on the 'Move2Learn' project (Wellcome Trust, ESRC, NSF) and has co-led several other research projects, most recently 'WeDraw' (EU H2020). Her recent publications include *Digital Bodies: Creativity and Technology in the Arts and Humanities*, with Sue Broadhurst (2017), and *The SAGE Handbook of Digital Technology Research* (2013), with Carey Jewitt and Barry Brown.

Nikoleta Yiannoutsou is a Research Fellow at the UCL Knowledge Lab, University College London. Her research interests lie at the intersection of education, psychology, design and technology studies, including the design and evaluation of emerging technologies (multisensory technologies, robotics, mobile technologies and digital games) for learning. She has been a Research Fellow on a number of projects, most recently 'WeDraw: Exploiting the Best Sensory Modality for Learning Arithmetic and Geometrical Concepts Based on ICT Multisensory Technologies and Serious Games' and 'ER4STEM (EU) Educational Robotics for STEM'. Her recent publications include *Exploring How Children Interact with 3D Shapes Using Haptic Technologies*, with Johnson and Price (2018).

List of Figures

Chapter 1
Introduction: Digital Touch Communication

Abstract In this chapter, we make a case for the significance of touch for communication and suggest that developments in sensory digital technologies are bringing touch to the fore in ways that move digital communication beyond 'ways of seeing' to include new 'ways of feeling'. We argue that this shift requires us to take new measure of digitally mediated touch, or 'digital touch', as a communicational resource, what it is and can be, how it is designed and imagined, and its communicative potentials and limitations. We situate digital touch communication in relation to a technological awakening to a broader social revaluing of people's sensorial experience. We introduce and reflect on the socially orientated stance to digital touch we take in this book, and the InTouch project more generally. The chapter provides an overview of the book which also serves to introduce the key themes that it explores, that is the research and technological terrain of digital touch, social norms of touch, presence and connection, sociotechnical imaginaries of digital touch, and the ethics of touch. Finally, we introduce six InTouch case studies which examine digital touch across different contexts, perspectives and participants. We draw illustrative examples from these (alongside extensive engagement with the research literature) in order to enliven and consolidate the book's exploration of the sociality of digital touch communication across different contexts.

Keywords Touch capacities · Touch practices · Art · Parental touch · Designing touch · Tactile emoticon · Digital touch · Remote touch · Virtual touch

1.1 Introduction

Touch has a central role in the construction of our experiences and understanding of the world, ourselves and one another (Bull et al. 2006). We discuss why touch matters, and how the digital remediation of touch may inaugurate and develop new ways of feeling. We situate this book on digital touch communication within a broad

C. Jewitt et al., *Interdisciplinary Insights for Digital Touch Communication*, Human–Computer Interaction Series,
https://doi.org/10.1007/978-3-030-24564-1_1

social revaluing of sensorial experiences and the senses, a technological awakening to the sensory. This book comes out of ongoing work from InTouch: Digital Touch Communication, the five-year project (funded by the European Research Council), introduced in this chapter. We close the chapter with an overview of the book chapters and sketch the social themes addressed across the book.

1.1.1 *Touch Matters*

Touch is the first sense through which humans apprehend their environment and it is central to our development (Field 2003). Touch may not be much spoken about, yet it provides significant information and experience of the world; it is crucial for tool use (Fulkerson 2014) and is central to communication: 'Just as we 'do things with words' so, too, we act through touches' (Finnegan 2014: 208). Indeed, knowing how to infer meaning from touch is considered the very basis of social being (Dunbar 1996). It is significant for developing and maintaining personal relationships, from ritualized greetings, to communicating emotion or intimacy (McLinden and McCall 2002), and is an effective means of influencing attitudes, creating bonds between people, places or objects (Krishna 2009), and improving information flow and compliance (Field 2010).

1.1.2 *Digital Touch*

Advances in the design of digital touch and the importance of touch in communication require social science and designers to understand its place in the sociality of interaction. Throughout this book, we use the term 'digital touch' to emphasize our attention to the social orientation of touch and to refer to the digital-mediation of touch by a broad range of technologies, beyond the hand. We prefer 'digital touch' rather than 'haptic' which references a technological or physiological orientation and are strongly linked to the hand via its etymological roots 'grasping'. Digital touch communication can be co-located or remote, and might involve human-object, human-human, human to robot or robot to human touch.

The importance of touch in human development has long been recognised (e.g. Fisher et al. 1976), however, this sensory feature of human communication is only recently pervading the digital landscape. Digitally mediated touch matters, it is considered within computer science and HCI to have the most potential of the senses for digital communication and it is the sense most rapidly being developed in the intensification of digital sensory communication (Hoggan 2013) (while technologies to synthesise and exploit taste and smell are emerging, their potential for communication is as yet unclear). The proliferation of digital devices that have escalated communicational capacity through audible, written and visual modes, have also foregrounded debates around touch deprivation. These have been critiqued for reducing or removing touch from the communicational environment, and the limitations of devices to date that support affective touch, which typically focus only on the hand or forearm (Huisman 2017). Whilst acknowledging our everyday interaction with touch screens, our focus in this book is on emergent and semi-speculative touch technologies that want us to be able to touch and feel objects in new ways: from tangibles, wearables, haptics for virtual reality, through to the tactile internet of skin. Developments in haptic, sensor and touch-related technologies, point to technological opportunities to develop and enhance our touch interaction and communication. The perceived value of integrating tactile qualities to digital devices, systems and interaction is considerable, given that touch is critical for our physical and emotional well-being (van Erp and Toet 2015), social development and social communication (Field 2010). More critically, tactile technological 'innovation' speaks to the 'always on', 'hyper-attentive' subject 'disciplined for tactile calls to attention, a body open to these calls to be productive at all times' (Parisi and Farman 2019: 3).

Across a range of social contexts and technological domains, touch-based technologies promise to supplement, heighten, extend and reconfigure how people (and machines) communicate, leading to new touch-based capacities and practices. However, this raises significant technical challenges for engineering, computer science and robotics, requiring detailed research into areas such as understanding mechanical touch and physiological touch. It requires complex developments in exploring optimal ways to make robot hands move, for example, or how to build and programme how to 'sense', for example through 'skin', raising the need to solve issues of creating 'senses' not typically present in technology. Alongside these technical drivers of touch-based technologies there are a number of social drivers. Changes in 'globalisation' have led to more 'distant' relationships – family, friends and romantic partners– generating a perceived demand for generating physical sensations across a distance, extending the 'touch' channel of communication remotely. Opportunities to enhance the quality of life for people with a disability or sensory loss (e.g. of vision) bring digital touch capacities into rehabilitation and prosthetics. Within robotics the need to develop touch awareness and touch capacity in robotic agents for teleoperation contexts is essential for enhancing robot capability in undertaking delicate operations, such as bomb disposal, and in health care contexts, where robot touch need to effectively convey emotion or meaning through touch, and interpret emotion or meaning through touch. These socially oriented considerations are drivers for technical development and underpin the design and development of many emerging digital touch technologies.

1.2 Situating This Book: A Social Revaluing of the Sensory and Multimodal

Our exploration of digital touch communication is situated within a broad social revaluing of people's sensorial experience and re-evaluation of the roles of the senses, a part of which is a technological awakening to the sensory. Digital touch can be related to changing social configurations (produced through the global economics of work and migration for example), that generate a desire and/or need to achieve digital immersive connection with others at a distance, as well as the possibilities of technological innovation. This is driving a new wave of digital sensory communication devices and environments. In light of this we approach digitally mediated touch as a communicative mode (albeit one in a state of flux and development), and a sensorial experience entangled in the materiality and sociality of the body, the environment and technologies.

Our concern with the sociality of digital touch, in this book, and InTouch more generally, provides an alternative starting point to the physicality of touch. While the body remains at the heart of our thinking, we move away from a concern with mechanisms and processes of perception, the senses as a universal biological-physiological matter of information-processing, physical realizations (the brain and the body systems), and the relationship between stimuli and the sensations and perceptions they affect. Rather than, for instance, approaching the skin as an organ, to explore its sensory receptors (nerve endings and corpuscles), we approach it as "lived as both a boundary and a point of connection…the place where one touches and is touched by others; it is both the most intimate of experiences and the most public marker of raced, sexed and national histories" (Ahmed and Stacey 2001: i). Similarly, when we explore the memories and emotions that touch evokes for people, our concern is at the level of their social and sensorial experiences, rather than at that of tactile perception and the somatosensory activity and processes of the brain (Spence and Gallence 2014). This is not to dismiss the physiology of the body, but rather to draw attention to the socially shaped and interpreted sensorial experiences of the body, specifically of touch, and to argue that these different levels of bodily meanings are always in conversation always, always becoming, as "the interfaces between bodies and their worlds are made and unmade through social practices" (Scarry 1985: 5).

The sensory and the social are paramount in the development of digital touch devices and environments in ways that point both to the 'shifting, contingent, dynamic and alive' character of the senses, specifically in this case, touch (Jones 2007: 8), and the ever-closer relationship between the sociality of touch, technology and sensory communication. This shift poses a challenge for research and design to illuminate touch communication, particularly given that the social sciences have a patchy relationship to touch, beyond a few references to touch within seminal communication studies (e.g. Goffman 1979; Simmel 1997; Bourdieu 1986). This work provided an early basis for the sociological and cultural turn to the body, the interdisciplinary foundation for sensory studies (Bull et al. 2006), and the sociology of the senses (Vannini 2015). Similarly, in Human Computer Interaction (HCI), the Somatic Turn (Loke and Schiphorst 2018), a part of Third Wave HCI, has resulted in interdisciplinary and mixed methods research that reflects upon the body.

While interest in embodiment is not new, most socially orientated methodological strategies that attend to the body continue to be inadequate for getting at the social aspects of touch as they are primarily based on talk alone. In addition, despite the interdisciplinary turn to the multimodal and the sensory, and the increased centrality of embodiment and materiality, touch has, with a few notable exceptions (Classen 2005, 2012; Finnegan 2014), been neglected by both multimodal and sensory scholars. Cultural and media studies has brought touch into focus through touch metaphors and haptic visuality (Marks 2002; Cranny-Francis 2011), although the newly emergent Haptic Media Studies provides a historical and philosophical grounding for the study of touch as it is digitally mediated (Parisi et al. 2017). Despite these new developments, however, touch communication is not well understood at a crucial moment when its extension into the digital realm raises new questions for social interaction and development.

1.3 InTouch Digital Touch Communication

This book provides a snapshot of the authors' ongoing work on InTouch: Digital Touch Communication. InTouch is a five-year project (funded by the European Research Council) which explores the social implications of digital touch technologies for communication, with the aim of enhancing socially orientated understandings, research and design of digital touch. We seek to anticipate and confront the social, political and ethical challenges raised by digital touch (e.g. privacy, safety, and digital exclusion); to enhance our capacity to fully imagine and engage with the social relevance and potential of digital touch for communication; and to support the development of digital touch devices, systems and environments that take adequate account and care of people's communicative practices and social contexts. We examine digital touch across various contexts of communication and technologies, from future speculation to bio-sensing to robotics. In particular, our research is grounded on a number of key research areas related to understanding and designing digital touch.

We examine how touch is conceptualized, imagined and experienced by people through different technologies and in different contexts. We investigate the aspects of digital touch (e.g. physical, emotional, social) that are central to a range of communicational situations; explore how people improvise around digital touch; review the skills, experiences and communicative repertoires that they draw on/or speculate they will use for digital touch to communicate; and explore how they experience and imagine connection/connectivity, social relations and emotions, being experienced or communicated through digital touch.

We are interested in how designers and users take up the resources of touch that are available to them. In particular, we attend to what sensory-affective qualities and affordances, and the materiality of different touch technologies feature in different social and situated contexts; we explore how designers and users (re)appropriate touch technologies for the purposes of communication and the sensory concepts and categories that they employ, evoke, and imagine in their development of digital touch technologies.

We seek to understand the role of digital touch technologies for communication: how it might supplement, heighten, extend or reconfigure touch and touch communication. We are interested in how digital touch technologies are situated and embedded in the wider contexts and experiences of everyday life, and how touch technologies ask (require) people to reimagine these for the future.

1.4 Overview of the Book

In this section, we provide an overview of the book chapters and sketch the social themes addressed across the book.

Chapter 2 introduces and reflects on the multimodal and sensory and interdisciplinary methodological stance of this book, and the InTouch project more broadly. We introduce our main framework, which combines multimodality and sensory ethnography. We outline the collaborations and interdisciplinary dialogues that we have engaged with to explore digital touch, and argue that this approach brings different aspects of touch to the fore in ways that are productive for research and design. Finally, we then turn to discuss our use of prototyping as a way to gain access to and generate digital touch experiences and imaginations.

We begin to map the complex terrain of digital touch in Chap. 3, by drawing attention to key developments in digital touch capacity. This descriptive map of digitally mediated touch communication provides an overview of current state-of-the-art digital touch technologies, that enable new forms of touch communication in various contexts, such as work, leisure, learning, personal and social relationships and health and well-being. It is a 'history of now', that is, it outlines the conditions of the present state of digital touch technologies, on which the production of knowledge including understanding about the past and the future is itself contingent. It maps an array of digital touch communication research in relation to different communicative relationships: human-human touch, human-robot/robot-human touch, and human-object touch. We use these distinctions to help to raise questions and start debates about the interlinked nature of social issues that arise across these different communication spaces and contexts, whilst acknowledging that there is inevitably some overlap of the technologies/devices being developed and designed for use across these different contexts. This map documents the resources for touch, the touch interactions and communicative practices that are being designed for and starts to bring to the surface the social potentials and constraints of touch that are taken up by the designers of digital touch. Finally, the chapter, building on chapter two, provides an overview of the scope, extent and findings of user studies to date, and identifies emerging issues around the social aspects of digital touch communication, that might involve human-object, human-human, human to robot or robot to human touch.

The broader social debates that digital touch is situated within and emerges from are the focus of Chaps. 4, 5, 6 and 7. In these chapters, we attend to four topics: Social Norms, Connection and Presence, the Sociotechnical Imaginary and Ethics. While these are not the only topics that matter to understanding digital touch, they have repeatedly been to the fore across our case studies, the research literature, and conversations with others working within digital touch. They each show the potential of a socially orientated approach to research and design of digital touch, and the benefits of interdisciplinary research in this complex field.

We focus on social norms in Chap. 4, with attention to their significance for researching and designing digital touch communication in a global world, notably gendered and cultural touch norms. We explore how social and cultural norms shape the ways that people (and machines) touch. The ways in which touch norms are shaped, regulated and enforced through social, economic, familial and legal mechanisms, to organise our experiences and expectations is examined. We argue that understanding of the touch norms that people, including digital touch researchers and designers, bring to their interactions with others provides a route into understanding the sociality that informs digital touch. This is essential as the expectations of the user, their touch repertoires, and the social cultural norms in play in an environment shape the take up and use of mediated digital touch communication devices and systems and environments. This leads us to make a case for reflexive engagement with touch norms to provide insights and inspiration for thinking about, researching and designing digital touch communication, and to help to address how cultural and gendered norms of touch might be engaged with, to constrain and reproduce or open-up the meaning potentials of digital touch.

Technologies are intrinsically linked to the ways in which physical, temporal and emotional distances are thought of and managed. Likewise, social relations and communication technologies mutually shape each other as they are developed and maintained. Chapter 5 explores the social 'connections' that digital touch technologies are beginning to shape, with a focus on the related experiences of presence and absence through mediated touch and the questions this raises for the design space of interpersonal relationships, that is, the mediation of touch between people. We first consider how these concepts have been defined and addressed in the literature on communication technologies in general, and touch technologies in particular. We then use three case study vignettes to explore and reflect on these concepts. They include people's interactions and responses to a series of artistic technological provocations designed to enhance feelings of connection and tackle isolation in the 'Remote Contact' exhibition, an output of the *Art of Remote Contact* case study; the social aspects of sending and receiving digital touch as a form of tactile support, drawing on our study of people's use of a prototype *Tactile Emoticon*; and parents' use of the Owlet Smart Monitor (OSS), a bio-sensing baby monitor and app, which we conceptualize as a form of mediated touch in the context of parent-infant interaction in the *In Touch with Baby* case study. We consider how touch technologies might challenge us to think about the interaction between human and machine. We close with a consideration of design implications and possibilities for future research.

Chapter 6 explores the potential of the concept of sociotechnical imaginaries for digital touch communication research and design. It discusses and defines the social imaginary and how it works to produce and animate shared systems of meaning and belonging that guide and organize the world, in its histories as well as performed visions of desirable futures through advances in science and technology and imagined technological possibilities. The chapter explores the ways in which this concept can be employed as both a design resource, and as a methodological resource. We argue that as new digital touch technologies enter the communicational landscape the setting for interpersonal sociability is/will be reworked. Looking across our case studies, we explore and make legible emerging sociotechnical imaginaries of digital touch, asking how might touch practices be changed through the use of technology, and how might this shape communication. In particular, the chapter explores the core themes of the body, time, and place in relation to participants' sociotechnical imaginations of digital touch. Turning our attention to the sociotechnical imaginary as a methodological resource, we describe our use of a range of creative, making and bodily touch-based methods to access participants' sociotechnical imaginaries of digital touch and to both explore and re-orientate to the past, present and futures of digital touch communication.

Chapter 7 examines key ethical considerations and challenges of designing and researching touch technologies, with a focus on incorporating ethical touch sensitivities and values into digital touch communication. We discuss the difficulty of researching and designing ethically in the context of an emerging technological landscape, as reflected in wider HCI ethics debate. The chapter then explores the central role of the human body as site for digital touch communication, before focusing on key challenges around trust, control, consent, and tactile data. In line with preceding chapters, we draw on our case studies and the literature, to argue that digital touch practices are part of, and impact on, wider social relations and communications. The kinds of touch practices and relations designed *into* touch technologies bring with them implications for power relations and social cohesion, and it is these wider processes that digital touch design is able to – at least in parts – anticipate and shape. We close with a summary of key points and their implications for research and design.

Chapter 8, closes the book with a note on closing thoughts in response to the speculative and emergent character of digital touch communication, signalling our desire and need to keep the conversation open. We point to the significance of a social take on digital touch, particularly with reference to the types of questions this perspective raises and the way it positions technology in relation to people and society more generally. We draw attention to the research insights on digital touch communication discussed throughout the book that may inform design. Finally, we comment on the theoretical and methodological routes that we have taken to research digital touch communication; and draw on the ideas and research presented in this book to sketch an emergent research and design framework for digital touch communication.

1.5 InTouch Case Studies

In this section, we introduce the six case studies that we refer to and draw examples from in this book. Each case study is designed to examine project research themes discussed earlier, and to explore the different ways in which touch is conceptualised, how it is materialised and operationalised in different contexts and for different purposes, as well as how it is situated within the broader sensorium and with other media. The case studies draw attention to the social uses of digital touch, the losses and gains of touch for meaning making and communication, the reshaping of touch practices, as well as showing some of the ways that touch 'stands in for' or gets 'translated' into other representational and communicative modes in digital designs. Each case study is outlined below.

1.5.1 *Imagining Remote Personal Touch*

Digital technologies have increased the potential for establishing, developing and maintaining relationships at a distance, through the configuration of key concepts, such as mobility, interactivity, temporality, social cues, storage, replicability, reach, and materiality (Baym 2015; Madianou and Miller 2012). As geographical distances increase, online communication increasingly supports an 'always on' culture of ubiquitous connectivity that allows 'a new type of connected family at a distance' (Madianou 2016: 184). Touch is increasingly being designed into digital communication devices/interfaces, with remote personal relationships becoming a primary market domain. When a new technology enters the 'technoscape', societies reach a consensus through an etiquette on their use and, over time, develop a set of norms (Licoppe 2004). Given the embryonic stage of digital touch devices, the norms for digital touch use are in a state of flux, most devices are un-domesticated, unstable and in labs rather than 'in the wild', making observing their everyday use impossible. Nonetheless, as with the history of other technological developments we know that the development of digital touch communication will be shaped by a sociotechnical imaginary. This case study explores how we begin to capture what that sociotechnical imaginary about digital touch is.

The case study revolved around three research workshops designed to explore future possibilities for digital touch design for personal remote communication in three fields: friendships, family, and/or intimate partnerships. Our aim was to not only explore design ideas, but to also better understand key socially oriented considerations when designing for touch forms of communication, such as, where on the body can be touched, who can touch, how can we touch, and how norms of privacy and power relationships shape touch imaginaries. An interdisciplinary and multicultural group of 31 participants were recruited, to capture a range of perspectives on personal communication relating to distance and the digital. The first workshop activity was designed as a brainstorming session focusing on participant histories and experiences of remote digital communication in general, discussing continuities and change over the last 10 years. The second activity was a rapid prototyping session, described in the previous section (Fig. 1.1). Kissenger (Zhang et al. 2016), a working remote communication device, was the basis of the third workshop activity, in which it was used as a 'disruptive probe' to explore participants' interactions and reactions, and reflections on an existing digital touch communication device.

Fig. 1.1 Rapid prototyping sessions and prototypes in the Imagining Remote Personal Touch Case Study

A combined multimodal (Jewitt et al. 2016; Kress 2010) and sensory ethnography (Pink 2015) approach to the analysis showed five thematic characteristics around digital touch for remote communication, namely: materiality (e.g. in terms of loss of particular sensations expected of touch, like warmth), embodiment (whole body sensation versus specific body location for communicating touch), post-human aspects (e.g. concerns over loss of emotional and sensorial aspects of communication through machinic touch), emplacement (e.g. appropriate space/places for touch communication), and digital touch temporalities (e.g. attending to questions of duration of touch experience, social timing of touch, storage of and asynchronous touch experience), all of which provide insights on the emerging landscape for digital touch personal communication (Jewitt et al. under review).

1.5.2 In Touch with Baby

This case study focuses on bio-sensing technology to explore the potential new conceptualisations of 'digital touch' that this brings about. Proliferation of bio-sensing technologies in various contexts remediates bodily and physiological information through the 'touch' of the device on the skin, or even as an implant, to bring

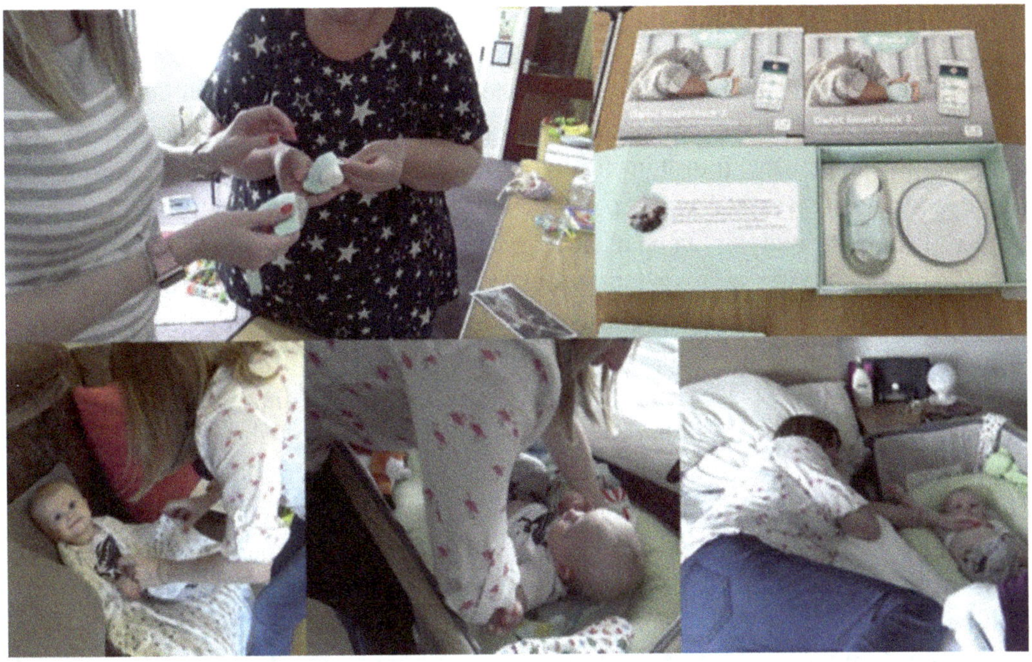

Fig. 1.2 The Owlet Smart Sock and bedtime re-enactments, In Touch with Baby case study

new awareness of our own or others' bodies, with information commonly derived through touch, e.g. taking a pulse, or temperature. We focus on the Owlet Smart Sock (OSS) baby monitoring device (designed, developed and marketed by Owlet), which detects babies' real-time heart rate and oxygen levels, and alerts caregivers if readings fall outside the norm (Fig. 1.2). We view this bio-sensing technology as digitally mediated touch, in part due to the contact of the smart sock on babies' skin, and in part through wireless transmission of physiological data to parents' smart phones, imparting information about the baby's physiological state and well-being. Different from other case studies, the use of a ready-for-market technology enabled InTouch to explore the use of a stable touch-related device 'in the wild', with the full use of its accessibility, and connotations and status for the public.

The study focuses on how the technology may interact with or reshape the ways in which parents and babies communicate, know and experience each other through touch – especially given the role of parental touch in assessing baby's temperature, breathing, body tone, through for example, laying a hand on the baby's back or chest while sleeping. Specifically, this technology raises socially orientated questions about how parent/child touch is digitally mediated through early parenthood, and to what social, sensory-affective and communicative consequences; how the use of digital touch technologies (bio-sensing baby monitors) co-constitute and reimagine babies' and parental bodies, their boundaries and (biological and/or physical, cultural and social) connections; how the technological design maintains, interprets, disrupts or generates new touch and sensory-affective practices and routines in parenthood.

The case study drew on ethnographic approaches and comprised a number of stages. Focus group discussions, involving a total of 13 participants in parent-group formats, provided insights into parental touch practices with their babies, and their initial perceptions of the potential or value of the Owlet technology, or similar devices. Subsequently, four families volunteered to take the Owlet Smart Sock home and use it over a 3-week period. Sensory ethnography methods combined with multimodal analysis were used to generate qualitative data in the homes of participants, involving semi-structured interviews and bedtime video re-enactments. The trialling of the technology was accompanied by participant-led WhatsApp updates across the use period, and a subsequent reflective interview explored the Owlet experience post-use. This allowed us to investigate the perceptions of connection and communication that the device afforded parents who used it with their babies, specifically relating these to touch-based practices, and implications for any changing touch-related communication.

Along with the focus group discussions, the video re-enactments highlighted the ways in which touch is dispersed across, situated and made meaningful in family routines and wider everyday activities, which in itself problematizes the notion of 'replacing' human touch. We found the OSS to enter an already existing ecology of home that contains other technologies, bodies, material contexts, and wider sensory environments. Parents adopted, adapted or rejected the device as part of their wider roles and responsibilities as caregivers, actively negotiating OSS readings with their own sense of baby's well-being. The OSS was most disruptive where it could not slot into existing practices of parent-infant touch interaction, and most revealing where the sensor readings enabled parents to make sense of their babies' bodies and activities (e.g. falling asleep) in new ways.

1.5.3 The Art of Remote Contact

The ways in which touch technologies are designed can change the types of touch we can give/receive, and the ways in which we can communicate through touch, which raises interesting questions about what these might look like, and how people might use them. Communication technologies, like the phone, enable you to leave a voice message, and even record video messages – but what if you reached out to touch someone, and could leave a touch message? How might it be recorded and what would the life of that message be? In what contexts or situations might this be beneficial?

This case study was a collaboration between the interactive artist studio Invisible Flock and InTouch. The aim was to design and develop a series of interactive digital artefacts to engage people with touch, and creatively explore ways of enabling 'touch messaging'. The artworks explored the theme of facilitating different kinds of interaction at the level of touch between people with dementia, their friends and families, as verbal communication was difficult. We explored how a social science research project, can engage with artists, the digital artefacts that they make, and

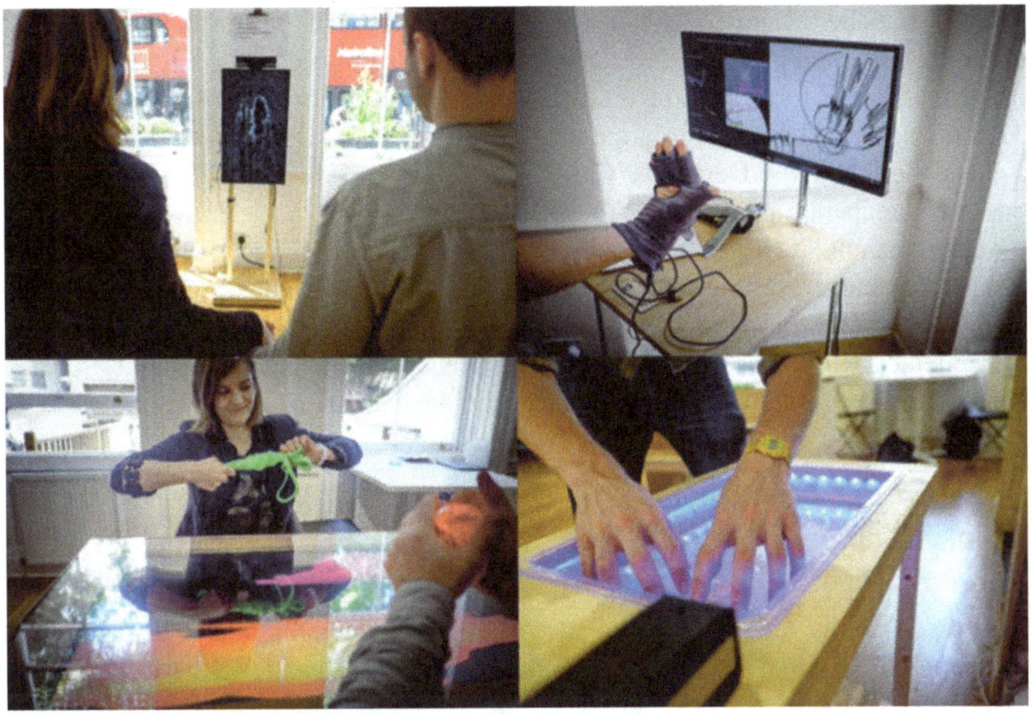

Fig. 1.3 Art of Remote Contact case study four exhibition artefacts. (Photo credit: Ed Waring)

their practices, to research digital touch communication as the 'new interpreters of digital innovation'. InTouch used ethnographic methods to document the development of the artefacts over a year, this included meetings, sharing links, papers, and photographs, studio-visits, in-progress demonstrations, interviews and the process of developing the exhibition. This enabled us to situate the exhibition and artefacts in a broader understanding of the histories, ideas and processes that informed its development.

The works formed an artistic research exhibition, Remote Contact, which was open to the public (Fig. 1.3). We also used the exhibition as a research environment to explore how members of the public who visited it engaged with the artefacts and one another. We conducted video walk-throughs with 31 visitors to the exhibition (lasting 30 to 90 min) to understand: the kinds of touch experiences, sensations and practices the exhibition invoked, provoked, supported and mediated for visitors; the touch resources and capacities visitors deployed; the cultural social norms, etiquettes, touch sensitivities that visitors articulated; as well as the memories, metaphors and experiences that visitors drew on to reflect on their touch experiences with themselves, others, and objects in the exhibition.

In this book, we use illustrative examples of visitors' interaction with three of the exhibition digital artefacts, which we briefly describe here. First, 'I wanna hold your hand' draws on how we communicate through the touch of hand holding, a squeeze, a stroke, to enhance experiences through durable re-representations. It included two separate artefacts, a pair of gloves and a 'Rain' installation. The 'Rain' installation made using Kinect, produced the sound of rain and a visual mapping of movement when visitors held hands. The pair of gloves map the walks of those holding hands, recording GPS and pressure, flex and galvanic skin response. This digital data from the gloves is transformed, using an Arduino plotter, into graphical drawings that can be kept and shared by users as a memory provocation. Second, 'Motion Prints' was a piece designed for Dementia Care Homes, to encourage physical interaction through therapeutic putty. A MYO arm-bracelet senses muscle movements while the users manipulate the putty, and this activity data is converted into a digital visualisation displayed on the table top. Third, the 'Water Synthesizer', involved the tactile sensation of moving water dynamically to create sounds related to the water movement. The online exhibition catalogue (Invisible Flock 2018) provides further context and information on these artefacts and the case study more generally.

1.5.4 Tactile Emoticon

This case study is a collaboration between the InTouch team, and UCL Computer Science, HCI Design and neuroscience. The Tactile Emoticon study aimed to explore the notion of 'tactile emoticons', building on ideas of visual emoticons used extensively in multiple communication contexts. The focus was on affective touch and how this could be digitally communicated between people remotely located. To do this we organised a workshop to explore the broad context of participants' engagement with emoticons and digital communication, and the role of different materials, sensory outputs and communication contexts for tactile emoticon messaging. Fifteen participants from Computer Science, HCI, Interaction design, Social science, Art and Design, and Neuroscience engaged in a brainstorming, participatory design activities, which aimed to explore tactile associations, and how different tactile materials might be used to create tactile messages associated to different emotions, for example, providing affective support through stroking.

The workshop results informed the iterative design and development of a prototype research device, configured to send and receive features of touch-based feedback, specifically heat, pressure and vibration to and from the hands of users. The prototype consisted of a mitten and a set of control buttons allowing synthesis of tactile messages by manipulating pressure, temperature and vibration (Fig. 1.4). Touch communication here takes place with and on hands.

A second workshop with 15 participants (postgraduate students and early career researchers, drawn from computer science, linguistics, communication and media studies), explored interaction with the initial prototype device. Two teams of two or three participants, situated in separate rooms (and unable to see one another), took turns in using the device to send and receive tactile messages. At the beginning of the session, they freely explored the device functionality and sensory features, then they engaged with tactile messaging (both sending and receiving) in the context of three different imagined scenarios: romantic love, social rejection and acute pain. In each of the scenarios the researchers assigned each team with one role, e.g. providing or receiving support or love, which was then reversed, so that all participants

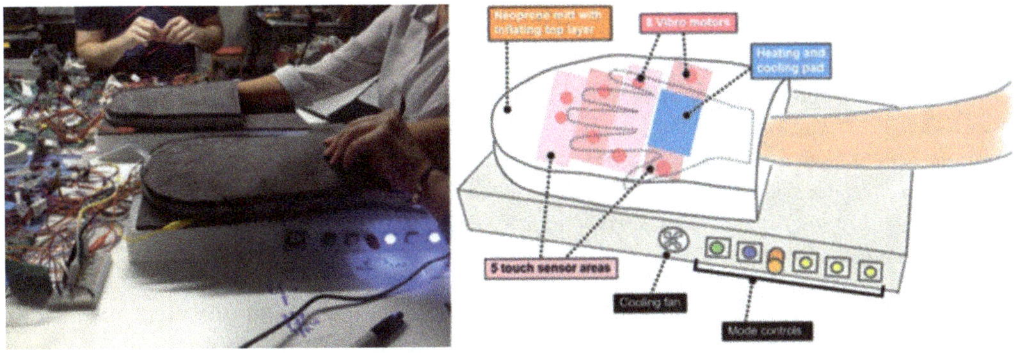

Fig. 1.4 The prototype Tactile Emoticon device, designed to send heat, pressure and vibration between the two 'mitt' sections. (Diagram credit: Frederik Brudy)

experienced being sender and receiver. This design had the potential for communicators to use the device to explore what meanings might be attributed to the different 'felt' sensations and develop their own 'language' of touch communication. The session concluded with a reflective discussion with both teams, aiming to inform the next design iteration.

The subsequent design prototype is being used in this collaboration as a research probe in a series of four on-going explorative qualitative studies with pairs of participants (including close friends, family, romantic partners, and students). The studies follow a three stage process of familiarisation and free-play with the device, using the device to communicate via touch in given scenarios, and a semi-structured interview covering a range of themes (e.g. agency, norms and expectations, experiences of connection/presence, memories and associations, and ambiguity) with each pair using video re-enactment of their experiences of interacting with the device, and to provide insight into the kinds of communicative messages they can send and interpret, the key aspects of touch sensations that enable this, and those that are less clear for communication.

1.5.5 Designing Digital Touch

Interviews and discussions with technical companies (e.g. HaptX) foreground the importance being placed on touch, the functional and useful designs for end users and highlight how technical companies are working within multidisciplinary teams to achieve this. Engagement with and awareness of these perspectives is essential for students studying digital design. We were interested to know how design students think about and through touch, and what happens when digital touch communication moves to the centre of the design process. To explore this, we collaborated with Design Educators, Dr. Val Mitchell and Dr. Garrath T. Wilson, at the Loughborough University School of Design and Creative Arts, to co-develop a student design brief for their BA and MA in Industrial Design and Technology, of which User Experience (UX) Design is an optional module.

Design Brief:

Develop an innovative, future-facing digital product or service that enhances communication through touch in one of three sectors: personal relationships, leisure, or health and well-being. To do this, you need to first research a specific communication context that would benefit from the introduction of touch technology, for face-to-face or remote interaction. You then need to identify specific user needs and, in collaboration with target users, develop and refine a product or service that will respond to those needs that includes an element of digital touch.

Students were encouraged to move beyond touch screens and mobile apps and to incorporate other forms of tangible interaction, existing or emerging technologies or those that could be considered as possible developments of current technological trends. While they could draw on other senses or modalities, touch was to be central to their design solution. We introduced students to the broad concept of digital touch communication and the kinds of technologies that may facilitate digital touch communication now and in the near future.

The research process involved following 70 students' work through a series of UX workshops (led by Val and Garrath), observing and video recording different design research and prototyping stages, and their associated coursework, which included storyboarding and video prototyping as well as on-going exchanges to collect learnings from Val and Garrath. (Students' participation in our study was voluntary and did not impact on their assessment.) The InTouch team reviewed and conducted a thematic analysis of their storyboards and video prototypes. We reflected on the kinds of design concepts that emerged and how the digital-touch-centred brief shaped the design process and located the students' concepts in the emerging landscape of digital touch and, in doing so, explored what types of touch resources are involved, where on the body touch is located, where and how communication happens, in relation to what other modes and senses. We examined the different ways in which the students brought the body into digital touch, from using it as an interface to something that can be sensed and differently known through the digital (e.g. through bio-sensing and wearable solutions), using touch technology as a sensory extension of the body or as sensory mediator between a person and their environment. From a social perspective, it is interesting for us to tap into the designers' imagination, to explore what narratives underlie their user scenarios, and what problems are solved through digital touch.

Designing digital touch is complex, and this led to the extension of the study to explore ways to prompt and support a border, more nuanced conception of digital touch. This resulted in the collaborative development of a prototype Designing Digital Touch Toolkit (Fig. 1.5) to support design students to go beyond technology-driven solutions by putting more emphasis on the sensory and communicative properties of touch throughout the design process, to encourage greater awareness, discussion and investigation of touch. It has been developed to support engagement with the complexities of working with touch across the Double Diamond model

Fig. 1.5 Designing Digital Touch Toolkit development

stages of Design Thinking. Our first toolkit prototype is being tested and evaluated by design students from a range of design courses. There are three types of cards for each stage: FILTERS- questions to help participants reflect on their own and others' experiences; WILD CARDS - deliberately abstract prompts for thought or action; and ACTIVITIES – more structured exercises which require some time. Initial work is presented in (Mitchell et al. 2019) and we will continue this collaboration to trace changes in the way touch technologies and design concepts are envisaged or employed across time.

1.5.6 Virtual Touch

This case study explores dimensions of touch in virtual and augmented reality environments – where experiences are classed as immersive or non-immersive. To date in immersive VR, typical touch interactions take place through pressing buttons or moving touch wheels on hand held wireless controllers. In some immersive VR experiences, 'touching' and eliciting changes in visual graphics is mediated through

Fig. 1.6 Instances of touch in Virtual and Augmented Reality. From left to right: Saatchi Gallery – We live in an Ocean of Air – VR Experience by Marshmallow Laser Feast; Discussion with Dr. Isabel Van De Keere, Founder and CEO of "Immersive Rehab"; Demonstration of an exoskeleton glove by Dr. David Swapp, Manager of the Immersive VR Lab at UCL, London

body movement (e.g. walking into different spaces or using gesture-like actions), and raise particular questions about touch in these spaces, for example, around the role of materiality, and relationship between 'virtual' touch and other representational modalities. However, developers are increasingly seeking other ways of enabling touch sensations in immersive VR, including haptic gloves using microfluidics to create different sense of pressure, simulating aspects such as weight, size, shape, texture (HaptX), or exoskeletal mechanics to deliver touch sensations, primarily through providing multiple points of force feedback arranged over a tracking glove (e.g. CyberGrasp). These devices are also designed for use in Augmented Reality environments, along with other haptic technologies, such as the Phantom, where touch sensations are felt through a pen-like tool in the form of vibration, and can be designed to elicit a sense of pressure or resistance; and non-contact technologies, such as mid- air haptics, which enable touch through ultrasound waves, giving sensations of shape and texture of three dimensional digital objects. While developers are increasingly advocating the potentials of haptically mediated touch devices for enhancing VR experiences or training capacities (e.g. in medicine), critiques highlight that these technologies are not yet mature enough to operate reliably outside lab settings (Stone 2019). Whether combined with haptic feedback or merely using body movement to engage in VR, the role of other media – visuals and audio – and modalities of interaction (e.g. gesture) are significant in conveying touch interaction or perceiving and interpreting touch interactions (Fig. 1.6).

Given the importance of touch in communication, designing for and embedding touch into VR contexts is challenging, and raises some important questions for understanding how touch is perceived and experienced in these spaces, and which specific designs enable these experiences. In particular, we are interested in environments where (physical) touch does not take place, what kind of touch sensations can the experience elicit e.g. prod, stroke, tap, and what this means for communication; how do people perceive, interpret or make sense of touch in these spaces, and what other resources do they draw on (e.g. context, visual) to achieve this, leading us to ask, what is the relationship between touch and gesture, and how does gestural interaction with virtual objects or graphics link to touch experience? In connection with this we are examining the role or importance of materiality, and how the materiality of interaction and communication change in different digital contexts. A further related question concerns the relationships between visual and tactile, or audio and tactile, and how can design foster effective touch perception through multimodal forms of representation.

To explore these questions, and better understand virtual touch from design to experience, we are engaging in four main research activities. First, we have conducted interviews, with (10) designers, developers, learning scientists, artists involved in the design, development and use of these technologies in different contexts, such as arts, education/training, healthcare, industrial design. This strand aims to look at aspects like what types of touch are afforded, to understand how designers and developers talk and think about touch in virtual and augmented spaces, why is touch important and in what scenarios, how touch is combined – supported with other senses, and where the norms of our non-digital touch practices are challenged. Second, we are analysing videos, audio and website texts presenting and or reflecting on VR and haptic applications, to examine how touch is talked about in the different experiences. Thirdly, in conjunction, we are analysing video walkthroughs of VR environments, where touch is featured as an important element, to examine how touch manifests in interaction and how it relates to current touch interactions with a view to exploring new forms of touch engagement. Fourth, we are undertaking a study of interaction in different VR environments employing touch forms of engagement as part of the experience and using different forms of input devices.

References

Ahmed S, Stacey T (2001) Thinking through the skin. Routledge, London

Baym N (2015) Personal connections in the digital age. Polity, Malden

Bourdieu P (1986) Distinction. Harvard University Press, Cambridge

Bull M, Gilroy P, Howes D, Kahn D (2006) Introducing sensory studies. Sens Soc 1(1):5–7

Classen C (ed) (2005) The book of touch. Berg, New York

Classen C (2012) The deepest sense: a cultural history of touch. University of Illinois Press, Urbane

Cranny-Francis A (2011) Semefulness: a social semiotics of touch. Soc Semiot 21:463–481

Dunbar R (1996) Grooming, gossip and the evolution of language. Faber and Faber, London
Field T (2003) Touch. MIT press, Massachusetts, MA
Field T (2010) Touch for socioemotional and physical well-being: a review. Dev Rev 30(4):367–383
Finnegan R (2014) Communicating. Routledge, London
Fisher JD, Rytting M, Heslin R (1976) Hands touching hands: affective and evaluative effects of an interpersonal touch. Sociometry 39(4):416–421
Fulkerson M (2014) The first sense: a philosophical study of human touch. MIT Press, Massachusetts, MA
Goffman E (1979) Gender advertisements. Harvard University Press, Boston
Hoggan E (2013) Haptic interfaces. In: Price S, Jewitt C, Brown B (eds) The Sage handbook of digital technology research. Sage, London, pp 342–358
Huisman G (2017) Social touch technology: a survey of haptic technology for social touch. IEEE Trans Haptics 99:1–1
Invisible Flock (2018) Remote contact. https://issuu.com/invisibleflock/docs/rc_booklet_issuu
Jewitt C, Bezemer J, O'Halloran K (2016) Introducing multimodality. Multimod Commun 5(2):1
Jewitt C, Leder Mackley K, Price S (under review) Emerging sociotechnical imaginaries of digital touch for remote personal communication. New Media and Society
Jones CA (ed) (2007) Sensorium: embodied experience, technology and art. MIT press, Massachusetts, MA
Kress G (2010) Multimodality: exploring contemporary methods of communication. Routledge, London
Krishna A (ed) (2009) Sensory marketing: research on the sensuality of products. Routledge, New York
Licoppe C (2004) 'Connected' presence: the emergence of a new repertoire for managing social relationships in a changing communication technoscape. Environ Plann D Soc Space 22(1):135–156
Loke L, Schiphorst T (2018) The somatic turn in human-computer interaction. Interactions:55–58
Madianou M (2016) Ambient co-presence: transnational family practices in polymedia environments. Global Netw 16(2):183–201
Madianou M, Miller D (2012) Migration and new media: transnational families and polymedia. Routledge, London
Marks L (2002) Touch: sensuous theory and multisensory media. University Minnesota Press, Minnesota
McLinden M, McCall S (2002) Learning through touch: supporting children with visual impairments and additional difficulties. David Fulton Publishers, London
Mitchell V, Wilson GT, Leder Mackley K, Jewitt C, Golmohammadi L, Atkinson D, Price S (2019) Digital touch experiences: educating the designers, CHI'19, Glasgow, Scotland, 04/05/2019. https://educhi2019.hcilivingcurriculum.org/wp-content/uploads/2019/04/p05-Digital-Touch-Experiences-Educating-the-Designers.pdf
Parisi D, Farman J (2019) Tactile temporalities: the impossible promise of increasing efficiency and eliminating delay through haptic media. Converg Int J Res New Media Technol 25:40–59
Parisi D, Paterson M, Archer JE (2017) Haptic media studies. New Media Soc 19(10):1513–1522
Pink S (2015) Doing sensory ethnography. Routledge, London
Scarry E (1985) The body in pain: the making and unmaking of the world. Oxford University Press, Oxford
Simmel G (1997) In: Frisby D, Featherstone M (eds) Simmel on culture: selected writings. Sage, London
Spence C, Gallence (2014) In touch with the future: the sense of touch from cognitive neuroscience to virtual reality. Oxford Uni Press, Oxford
Stone RJ (2019) Haptics for VR – where are we....really. https://www.linkedin.com/pulse/haptics-vr-ar-where-we-really-bob-stone?articleId=6512601603734847488#comments-6512601603734847488&trk=public_profile_post. Retrieved June 2019

van Erp JBF, Toet A (2015) Social touch in human computer interaction. Frontiers in Digital Humanities, Review, 27th May 2015
Vannini P (2015) Non-representational research: an introduction. In: Vannini P (ed) Non-representational methodologies: re-envisioning research. Sage, New York, pp 1–18
Zhang EY, Cheok AD, Nishiguchi S, Morisawa Y (2016) Kissenger: development of a remote kissing device for affective communication. Article 25. ACM

Links

Cybergrasp. http://www.cyberglovesystems.com/cybergrasp
HaptX. https://haptx.com/

Chapter 2
Interdisciplinary Explorations of Digital Touch

Abstract This chapter introduces and reflects on the multimodal, sensory and interdisciplinary methodological stance of this book, and the InTouch project more broadly. We introduce our main framework, which combines multimodality and sensory ethnography. We outline the collaborations and interdisciplinary dialogues that we have engaged with to explore digital touch, and argue that this approach brings different aspects of touch to the fore in ways that are productive for research and design. Finally, the different ways in which we use prototyping to gain access to, and to generate, digital touch experiences and imaginations for the purposes of research is outlined.

Keywords Digital touch · Interdisciplinary · Methodology · Multimodal · Prototype · Sensorial · Sensory

2.1 Introduction

As discussed in Chap. 1, the exploration of digital touch communication provided in this book is situated within a broad social revaluing of people's sensorial experience and re-evaluation of the roles of the senses, a part of which is a technological awakening to the sensory and changing social configurations to notions of connection, and possibilities for touch enabled through technological innovation. This is driving a new wave of digital sensory communication devices and environments.

We approach digitally mediated touch as a (emergent) communicative mode, a sensorial experience entangled in the materiality and sociality of the body, the environment and technologies. In this book, the sociality of digital touch is our starting point, rather than the physiology of touch to move away from a concern with sensory receptors, tactile perception and neurological processes. We understand the physical, material, and sensory aspects of touch as a part of when and how touch-based resources are taken up (or excluded) and how they can shape – or are shaped

C. Jewitt et al., *Interdisciplinary Insights for Digital Touch Communication*, Human–Computer Interaction Series,
https://doi.org/10.1007/978-3-030-24564-1_2

by – people to become semiotic resources. While, we draw insights on the dimensions of touch from a psycho-physical and neuropsychological account of the physical experience and perception of touch, these accounts are limited through their focus on the individual, understanding of the senses as universal (and somewhat 'fixed'), and not recognising "the role that culture plays in the modulation of perception senses function" (Howes 2011: 161). From our perspective, touch 'sensation' is much more than a biological and physiological process, insights on the physical dimensions of touch and the physiological processes through which 'signals' or tactile sensations (e.g. pain, temperature, pressure) are perceived are the 'stuff' of semiotics.

That digital touch communication is both a rapidly evolving area, and at the same time 'state-of-the-art' touch technologies are necessarily at an early stage of development and readiness, poses a number of methodological challenges for those who research it. In this chapter, we explore two such challenges.

First, the challenge of researching digital touch technologies that are unstable, lab-bound, and not yet domesticated. We have responded to this challenge of studying how people interact with such technologies, by using a range of methods and selecting a mix of technologies to enable 'naturalistic' interaction 'in the wild' to be observed; some early stable prototypes that can be demoed; alongside the lab-bound observation of unstable experiments and speculative early designs.

Second, the significant challenge of researching digital touch with underdeveloped methods and theories. We address this challenge through methodological innovation and an interdisciplinary approach using appropriate tools from multimodality, ethnographic tools attuned to the senses, art and design-based methods, and Human Computer Interaction (HCI) approaches. While multimodality and sensory ethnography provide the primary theoretical frame for this book, and InTouch more generally, our case studies all, albeit in different ways and to different extents, involve interdisciplinary collaboration and dialogue.

In the next section, we introduce our main framework, and make a case for our combination of a multimodal and sensory approach to the sociality of digital touch. We then turn to discuss our use of prototyping as a way to gain access to and generate digital touch experiences and imaginations and to support interdisciplinary dialogues on touch.

2.2 A Multimodal and Sensory Lens on Digital Touch Communication

Understanding bodily knowing through research on and with the body is a founding feature of the authors' work within multimodality (Jewitt et al. 2016; Jewitt 2014; Kress et al. 2005, 2014) and sensory ethnography (Leder Mackley and Pink 2014) especially as articulated in relation to digital communication and interaction (Jewitt and Price 2019; Price et al. 2016). We bring multimodality and sensory methods together to explore touch in response to the methodological challenge of how to understand the changing social landscape of touch, and the need for embodied methods to help gain insight on socially orientated understandings of digital touch. In this section, we offer a brief overview of multimodality and sensory ethnography (for a discussion of the challenges of doing so, see Jewitt and Leder Mackley 2018).

Within multimodality, objects and sequences of interaction are understood as meaningful signs – the outcome of a person's or people's actions, imbued with the maker's interests mediated through the environment in which the sign was produced or encountered (Kress 2010). Meaning is understood as socially situated choice from a (dynamic) set of available resources; the affordances of which are shaped through their historical, cultural and social usage and their materiality – all of which relate to and are shaped by technologies. Here we use affordance to refer to the idea that different modes offer different potentials for making meaning – a form of action. Modal affordances affect the kinds of semiotic work a mode can be used for, the ease with which it can be done, and the different ways in which modes can be used to achieve broadly similar semiotic work. Modal affordances are connected both to a mode's material and social histories, that is, the social purposes that it has been used for in a specific context.

Multimodality enables us to describe, categorize and understand the material and social resources and affordances of touch, the principles that underpin them, how they are shaped and used. For instance, how signifier materials (e.g. temperature, pressure, texture) are, through their social usage (the work of people, communities and societies), made into signs shared by a community and used to communicate, and to shape, establish or maintain social norms and conventions (e.g. notions of gendered touch, see Chap. 4). As an approach to communication it stresses the relationship between meaning systems and the social needs they are used to serve (Bezemer and Kress 2016; Kress 2010). InTouch uses a multimodal approach to ask what is counted as touch by participants in a given context, what semiotic meanings they associate with the dimensions of touch (e.g. location, temporality), and how these are used and interpreted by people to make meaning. For instance, placing one's hand on the shoulder of another person and holding it there for a long time, with pressure, to communicate intimacy and reassurance, or power and control (depending on the context). In this way, multimodality raises issues of power and agency, for instance in relation to who can touch. Using multimodality, we are starting to map the emergent dimensions of digital touch and the social conditions and contexts that shape it as well as to characterise people's use of touch for communication with attention to the cultural and social norms and power relations that shape their use (Jewitt 2017).

If multimodality asks how meaning is made and communicated, what meanings are made, and by whom, sensory ethnography sets out to account for the experiential, how meaning is perceived, the sensorial and often unspoken dimensions of everyday life and human activity (Pink 2015). It presents a set of phenomenological approaches that are attuned to people's sensory worlds and exist in theoretical-methodological dialogue with wider theories and concepts around human perception, place, knowing, memory, imagination, affect, and movement (Leder Mackley and Pink 2013). A key methodological feature of sensory ethnography is shorter-focused encounters with participants and the notion that much of what is important about our feelings and activities is not easily observed or put into language – tacit, embodied, and unspoken. This approach enables us to find routes through which to share or imaginatively empathize with the actions of people, collaboratively exploring with participants their ways of knowing, being and doing, whilst drawing on their own embodied and emplaced understandings (Dicks 2014). Video is used to generate ethnographic encounters in ways that account for their multi-sensoriality and functions, through a 'form of acquaintance rather than description' (Pink 2015: 2), as a way for the researcher to feel their way back into the research context. The video re-enactments used in our In Touch with Baby case study illustrate this 'empathetic encounter' with the participants' sensory worlds with an emphasis on understanding the place of touch.

The analysis of the case study data uses a multimodal and multisensorial approach to explore how participants know and tell through touch and bodily interaction. Our engagement with the case study videos as data begins through re-viewing the recordings as a team, making notes of interactional details and tensions, reflecting on our own embodied experiences of the research activities and materials, and revisiting and handling prototypes with attention to their sensorial and social properties. We examine when and how touch, the sensorial and materiality are brought into the scope/discursive space of making meaning, as a way to generate understanding of participants' conceptualizations and realizations of digitally mediated touch. This approach focuses in on the modal and sensory choices that people make to represent and communicate, how these choices are shaped by people's interests, social position and context, and seeks to understand the social implications of their choices for meaning, communication and knowledge. These conceptualisations and organisations of touch are understood as framed by social-cultural historical contexts as dynamic and changing over time under the influence of new social factors. In this way, analysis of digital touch communication is grounded in the broad social framing provided by both approaches to emphasize the social-cultural embedded-ness of digital touch and to capture the nuances of the lived sensory accounts that shape the digital design and use of touch.

2.3 Interdisciplinary Dialogues of Digital Touch Communication

InTouch brings multimodality and sensory ethnography into conversation with a range of other disciplines. The emergent state of digital touch communication often means it is not possible to observe these technologies in use in a naturalistic setting (e.g. the home). This is especially problematic for multimodal and sensory ethnography, which usually observe technologies in naturalistic or 'in-the-wild' contexts, in order to explore issues of agency and power through uptake and the domestication of technologies (Rogers et al. 2013). However, HCI, design and the arts can create new digital touch communication environments through making, speculative prototyping, staged scenario work, and generating artistic experiences, enable us as social scientists to investigate new forms or potentials of social touch.

Our case studies (see Chap. 1) involve an element of interdisciplinary working through a mix of research collaborations, workshops and events, the research literature, the use of mixed methods and on-going dialogue, notably with:

- Artists (e.g. *The Art of Remote Contact, Virtual Touch* case studies);
- Neuroscience (e.g. T*actile Emoticon*);
- Designers (e.g. *Designing Digital Touch* case study);
- HCI, computer science and engineering (e.g. *In Touch with Baby, Tactile Emoticon*, and *Virtual Touch* case studies);

This interdisciplinary mix is also reflected in the InTouch team, we have backgrounds in Art, Design, Fashion, HCI, Media and Communication Studies, Psychology, and Sociology. We seek to achieve a rich and nuanced account of digital touch communication, working across our methodological and conceptual differences to understand points of difference, and, where useful, how they can be productively brought into dialogue by contrasting and layering disciplinary understandings.

Disciplinary differences in where and how touch research takes place (Berker et al. 2006) offers potential for productive interdisciplinary collaboration. At a most basic level, we have had to explore how our different conceptualisations of touch and the digital: do we mean the same thing when we talk of touch? Each discipline has distinct, and sometimes incompatible conceptualisations of touch. These are embedded in disciplinary histories and methodological approaches. Within *Tactile Emoticon*, for example, whilst as social scientists, HCI interaction designers, computer scientists and neuroscientists we all understand touch as a complex phenomenon involving the body, brain, and the social environment, we conceptualise and research touch in ways that emphasise and attend to these elements differently. From a multimodal and multisensorial ethnographic approach, we account for a broad context of participants' engagement with emoticons and digital communication, and their semiotic and sensory interactions with the device and one another, always reading this in relation to social and cultural norms. The HCI and computer science researchers are focused on designing and understanding interaction between the users and the device. The neuroscience researcher approaches touch in relation to the individual, physical realizations (the brain and the body systems), mechanisms and processes of touch perception, and the relationship between stimuli and the sensations and perceptions they affect.

It has been useful for us to understand the different views of technology across our interdisciplinary conversations and collaborations: the extent to which the digital is foregrounded or valued, the expectations placed on it, and the sense to which technology is mutually shaped through its use. For example, Invisible Flock, collaborators in the *Art of Remote Contact* case study, described themselves as having an 'agnostic approach to technologies', sometimes working with stable consumer technology and sometimes using physical computing systems to prototype their own, and the importance of not having a 'default go-to technology…So we try to stay open to technology…the idea comes first". The technology is introduced at a later stage of their research process than, for example, was the case in the *Tactile Emoticon* study – which had specific communicative ideas underpinning the design and therefore suggested the technologies to be used at an early stage.

Where and how the social comes into researching touch, has been a central aspect of our interdisciplinary work on digital touch communication. In the case of the *Tactile Emoticon* case study, for instance, while we all engage with the social, we did so by focusing in on different levels of the social. The social is at the heart of a multimodal and multisensory approach and its conceptualisation of touch a form of communication realising and realised through the social functions of a society or group, which are always present at the level of the individual. While HCI is a broad field, it is inherently social in the recognition of the user and their relationship with a device or technology, and places them at the heart of its research, 'always looking at people and scenarios of use, not just how the person works' (Field-note). Our neuroscience colleagues engage with the social in relation to understanding what prior experiences or pre-existing beliefs participants may bring to an experimental context.

Across the other case studies, both the artists, and differently so, the designers critiqued the social expectations of touch. A member of Invisible Flock spoke of trying to create 'a digital layer of friction between these normal interactions to then perhaps begin a conversation around it. So, you make holding hands a little bit more complicated so that maybe you stop and think about it a little bit more and we can begin a new conversation.' In other words, they work to actively extend and problematize a felt social experience for a visitor, they seek to create a new social touch moment, while we as social scientists attempt to capture, interrogate and understand it. Our interdisciplinary collaborations with art, design and HCI to create such environments or experiences, enable us as social scientists to investigate new forms or potentials of social touch have proven invaluable: opening up discourses of touch, and prompting speculation and imaginaries on digital touch desires and futures.

2.4 Prototyping

The difficulties many people experience in articulating bodily experiences, imaginations, and tacit knowledge raise challenges for research (Tarr et al. 2017: 1). We bring prototyping into the frame of social science as a way to engage research participants in exploring touch and digital touch communication. As social researchers exploring the multimodal and multisensorial qualities of touch, the ways prototyping enable the body to play a central role in generating qualitative data are significant (Jewitt et al. 2019).

With its origins in product development within Engineering, Design, Computer Science, and Human Computer Interaction, prototyping has typically been concerned with developing 'an idea about a product, system, service or policy to meet human needs and devising a plan for executing that idea' (Binder et al. 2011). It is also associated with Design Thinking, which advocates for 'thinking with your hands' as a way of quickly and practically exploring an idea and the feasibility and development solutions, to pre-empt wasting time and money on something that might not work or might not be 'user' centred, in a quick, cost-effective and contextually aware way (Dunne and Raby 2013). The re-orientation of prototyping to high level concepts and ideas, rather than design products and skills, has enabled it to travel across the boundaries of engineering and design into the humanities and social sciences, including anthropology (Salazar et al. 2017), and more recently, sociology (Lupton 2018).

The methodological migration of prototyping to social research has partly been fuelled by a desire to research 'emerging and uncertain worlds' (Myers and Dumit 2011; Salazar et al. 2017), notably imagined digital futures, 'configuring future imaginaries that may not be expected to come to pass' (Lupton 2018: 5). We have found, this method aligns particularly well with researching the unstable, uncertain, future-facing technological devices and environments associated with digital touch. By bringing prototyping into the frame of multimodal and multisensorial work, we situate it within a wider move towards innovative and creative social science methods (Jewitt et al. 2017).

Our use of prototyping across the InTouch case studies suggests prototyping can serve as a point of connection, a bridge, across disciplinary differences to support interdisciplinary research in the emergent and provisional area of digital touch. We have used prototyping, in which digital touch technologies feature as a research resource, in four different ways:

- Observing participants from within HCI, engineering and industry demo their prototypes as part of an interview process
- Deploying existing prototypes as research probes
- Facilitating prototyping workshops with research participants
- Collaborating with artists and HCI designers to inform the design and build of digital touch prototypes and observing interaction with these designs

These approaches to prototyping varied in relation to the function of the prototype, who had access to it, who was involved in making, the material and/or technological resources involved, and the degree of conceptual or technological 'finish'. They provided an opportunity for case study participants, and us as researchers, to externalize unrefined concepts in material ways and, in the process, to identify and clarify key aspects of ideas, to make present new scenarios for digital touch communication, provoked questions and surfaced differences (e.g. in conceptualisations of digital touch and/or communication). The prototypes were reflected on, assessed, and refined, and provided a prop for participants (and researchers) to enact the experience of using a proposed artefact.

We found prototyping an effective research tool for exploring digital touch communication with participants from design, art, and HCI who are familiar with it, as well as with others with no prior design experience. The use of prototyping, in these different forms, helped to facilitate interdisciplinary dialogues and collaboration on digital touch communication across the social sciences, the arts, HCI and neuroscience.

The *Imagining Remote Personal Touch* case study, for example, used prototyping to explore the participants' experiences, memories and imaginations of remote personal digital (touch) communication. Participants were asked to prototype a remote digital touch device, environment or system for use in a personal relationship. The prototyping focused on the process of making, using a diverse collection of materials (silicon, leather, feathers etc.), objects and prompt words (a wall of touch words on post-it notes), aiming to foster creative explorations around different sensory touch interactions. Of key interest was how participants used their bodies in the generation of ideas, the making process and demo process, when asked to 'perform' how their prototypes might be used. In addition to focusing on the process, we approached the prototypes that participants produced as meaningful multimodal and multisensorial signs, material traces of thinking, decision-making: signs of digital touch. We reflected on our own embodied experiences of the workshops and materials, revisiting and handling participants' prototypes with attention to their sensorial and social properties. We focused in on the prototyping process, paying specific attention to how materials were brought into the making, in relation to which parts of the body, and to what consequences for the social implications of digital touch. In a separate workshop activity, participants also engaged with Kissenger, an existing prototype kissing machine (Zhang and Cheok 2016) as a technological probe. Participants' interactions with Kissenger sparked conversations on the appropriateness of digital touch communication in remote personal relationships, intimacy and sex. Overall, prototyping enabled us to engage with participants' sociotechnical imaginations of the materiality of digital touch, map imaginations of touch and technology to the body and digital touch technology interfaces (Fig. 2.1).

Prototyping featured in the *Designing Digital Touch* case study, a collaboration with User Experience (UX) lecturers at Loughborough Design School, in two ways: first, we co-facilitated a rapid prototyping session with 70 participating design students; second, we developed a prototype toolkit. Here, prototyping was part of a longer design process – a one-term module where students used a design brief to develop an innovative, future-facing digital product or service that enhances communication through touch for personal relationships, leisure, or health and well-being. Observations on the prototyping session provided ethnographic background and insights for the analysis of the students' final concept boards and videos. The case study research led us to develop a prototype – the Designing Digital Touch Toolkit (see Chap. 1). We prototyped the toolkit, a card-based resource using the Double Diamond Design model (Design Council 2007), using a mix of brainstorming, referencing research papers and experiences on touch and digital touch, re-enacting pedagogic design scenarios from the module with our UX collaborators, drawing on the analytical themes that we saw across the work of the cohort, and referring to specific student concepts. Both these uses of prototyping provided a powerful point of connection between our different approaches to digital touch, opening up and articulating the sociality and sensorality of touch into the UX design space for digital touch communication (Fig. 2.2).

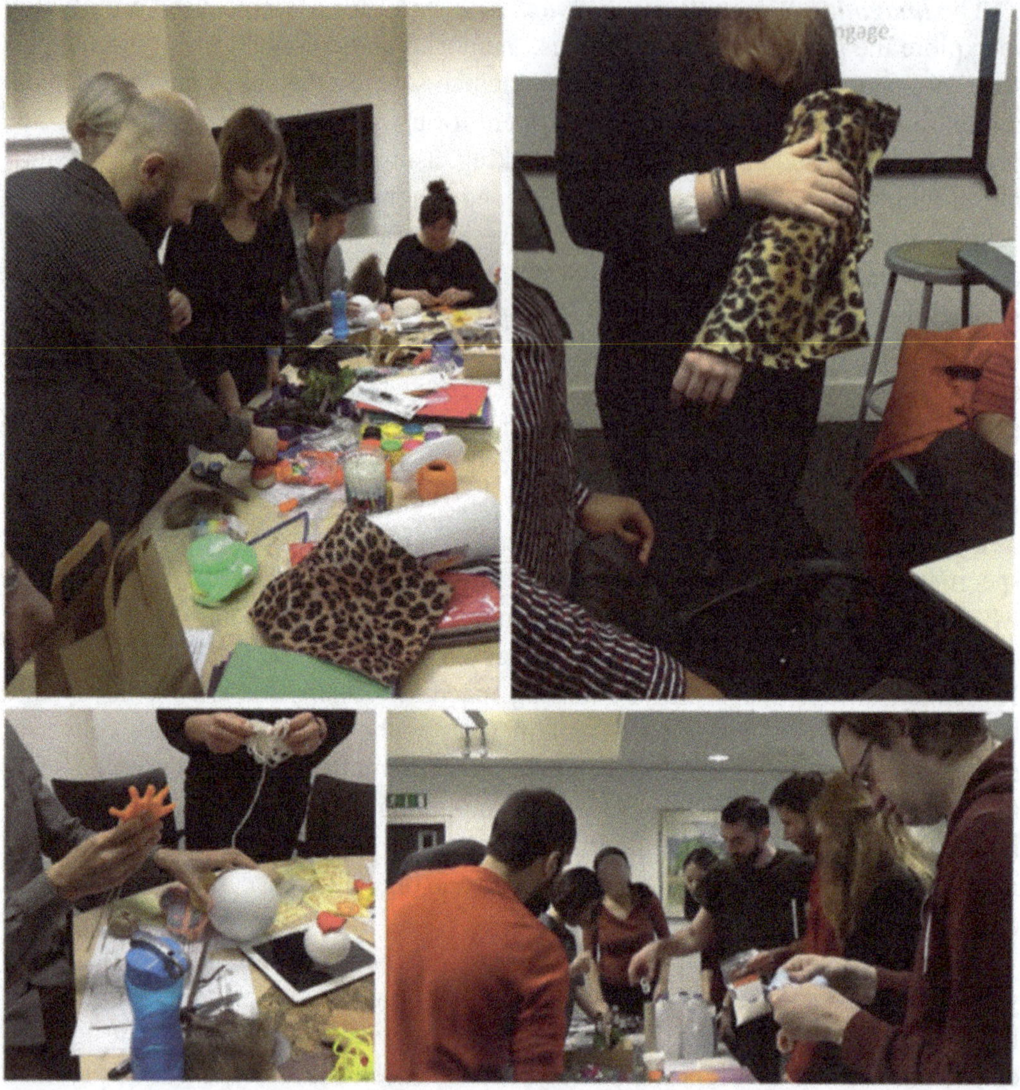

Fig. 2.1 Prototyping to explore participants' experiences, memories and imaginations of remote personal digital (touch) communication

The *Art of Remote Contact* case study used prototypes as research probes in the context of artistic practice-based research. Through ethnographic visits, demos and interviews we observed the artists' development of the prototypes, the decisions, ideas and processes involved in their making as well as sharing links, papers, photographs and ideas in the development process. Observing the development of the prototypes gave us useful insight on the artists' conceptualisation of touch, technology and digital touch. For instance, the prototypes, one of the artists explained, involved, "…taking existing tech and looking at them differently through a very human or poetic lens", rather than creating technology to "solve a specific problem or for commercialization". This stance created a very particular type of prototype,

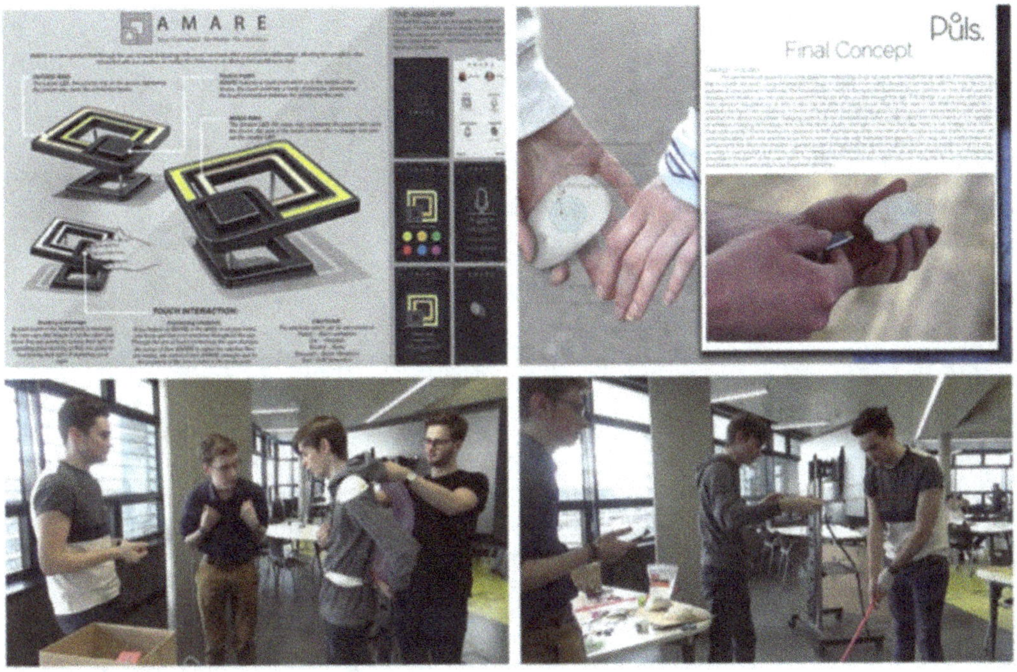

Fig. 2.2 Prototyping session as ethnographic background and insights for the analysis of Design students' final concept boards and videos. From top left to right: Amare by Betsy Cousins @betsyc_design; Puls by Joe Slatter https://www.behance.net/joeslatts82ca. Loughborough University design students exploring touch during rapid prototyping workshop

in contrast to the UX prototypes, designed to be unfinished without the visitor interaction. The prototypes were conceived as provocations, aiming to unsettle, generate friction with the seemingly familiar, to surprise, and to produce unpredictable tactile responses, rather than not 'art-works'. Their 'unfinished-ness' was signalled in its design through the use of plain wood frames and pedestals, off-the-shelf TV/computer screens, and the artistic decision to leave wires and plugs exposed making the technology visible to the gallery visitors. This use of low-fi materiality, rejecting the visual 'gallery-aesthetic' invited the audience to contribute to the prototype's completion through their interaction: invited them to touch. In this case study, prototyping generated a new digital touch environment, a public exhibition, for touchy exploration of digital touch communication, memories, experiences, and desires, as well contributing to exploration of the methodological potentials of collaborative working between social research and interactive art as research (Fig. 2.3).

The *Tactile Emoticon* case study was a collaboration with colleagues in neuroscience and HCI on the design and build of a prototype device to send and receive affective or socially supportive touch. The prototype device was designed to provoke interaction and imagined uses of digital touch interaction between two people. It sends touch feedback to the hands of two remote users using heat, pressure, and vibration, features of which were controlled by the sender. The design and development of the prototype device itself, and study participant responses and uses of it,

Fig. 2.3 Remote Contact exhibition, artistic provocations by Invisible Flock generate new digital touch experiences that can be observed and researched

informed the research. Prototyping, as a shared design and making activity, helped to elicit discussion on touch. The act of experiencing touch together was a generative process, helping to foster creative, unexpected and unpredictable conversations and ideas on digital touch. Research by doing and making, the iterations, failures and imperfect outcomes that we experienced, worked to expose our different conceptualisations of digital touch, our orientations to the social, and our expectations and requirements of digital technology. The iterative process of developing the prototype, its perceived utility and glitches, along with desires for further functionality and control, provided a space of interaction for us as researchers, as well as participants, and the final prototype functioned as a research tool for studies within our different disciplines. The social science and HCI researchers undertook qualitative studies with the device, exploring participants free-play with it, their responses to a series of scenarios, and the 'languages' of touch communication that participants

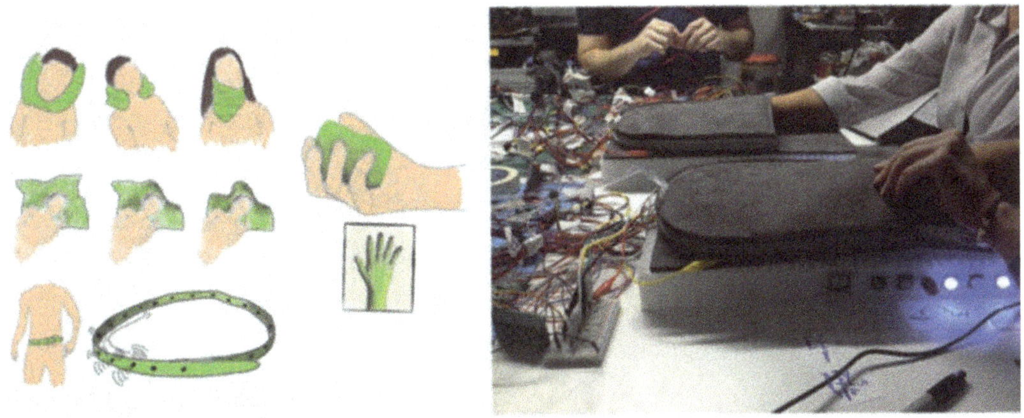

Fig. 2.4 Iterative prototype development by Frederik Brudy as part of the *Tactile Emoticon* case study

developed. Alongside this, a controlled, quantitative neuroscience study validated the tactile emoticon device to identify the affective responses to digital touch communication provided via the device. The prototype informed the development of design considerations for digital touch devices and future work (Fig. 2.4).

Within the *Virtual Touch* case study, prototypes provided a useful point of connection between expert developers within HCI, engineering and industry and us as social researchers. Several experts demonstrated their prototypes as part of the interview, for example, in the context of a VR rehabilitation environment, the designer invited the researcher to be in the role of patient and she, the designer, took the role of physio, talking the researcher through the tactile basis of her experience – the type of grip required, the level of pressure to use and so on, while the researcher challenged and experimented with the affordances of touch available to her: together they re-enacted the user situation through touch which provided a felt basis for the interview. Another expert used various prototypes (e.g. an exoskeleton glove and a robotic arm) in the interview to demonstrate their touch affordances, functions and limitations, and to highlight the "gaps of human perception" that design and engineering capitalize on to create a "realistic sense of touch". While in another interview, we used our experience of the technology to prompt questions to the expert, to clarify and elaborate the touch potentials of the virtual touch afforded, and to specify and concretise the abstract concepts that were raised in interview. By attending to the different ways in which the experts utilised their prototypes in the interviews we conducted, what they brought to the fore, enabled us to move beyond the virtual technology to gain insight on the narratives, social questions, and contexts of use that informed their work on virtual touch (Fig. 2.5).

Sharing and exploring concepts with collaborators from other disciplines through processes of making, touching, and manipulating materials and objects promoted collaborative interdisciplinary dialogues and thinking towards gaining new knowledge about relevant phenomena (Camburn et al. 2017): in this case, digital touch.

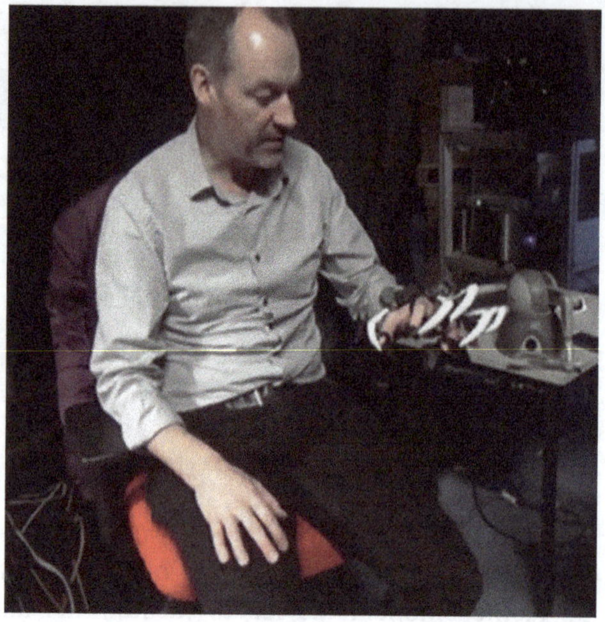

Fig. 2.5 Dr. David Swapp, Manager of the Immersive VR Lab at UCL, London, demonstrating touch affordances of an exoskeleton glove

2.5 Conclusion

This chapter has made the case for making the sociality of digital touch our starting point and the focus of this book. We have discussed the methodological challenges of researching digital touch communication at a time when technologies are evolving rapidly and are not yet 'domesticated', and methods and theories remain underdeveloped. Throughout the chapter, and the book more generally, we have argued for the need to attend to the multimodal and multi-sensorial aspects of touch and the significance of interdisciplinary dialogues with, for instance, art, neuroscience, HCI, and design. We have made the case for an approach to digitally mediated touch as a communicative mode, a sensorial experience entangled in the materiality and sociality of the body, the environment and technologies. We have discussed the potential of four different uses of prototyping to bridge interdisciplinary differences in order to gain access to and generate digital touch experiences and imaginations for research purposes. In the next chapter, we map the complex terrain of digital touch technologies for communication.

References

Berker T, Hartmann M, Punie Y, Ward KJ (2006) Domestication of media and technology. Open University Press, Maidenhead

Bezemer J, Kress G (2016) Multimodality, learning and communication: a social semiotic frame. Routledge, London

Binder T, De Michelis G, Ehn P, Jacucci G, Linde P, Wagner L (2011) Design things. The MIT Press, Cambridge, MA

Camburn B, Viswanathan V, Linsey J, Anderson D, Jensen D, Crawford R, Otto K, Wood K (2017) Design prototyping methods: state of the art in strategies, techniques, and guidelines. Des Sci 3:E13

Design Council (2007) Eleven lessons: managing design in eleven global companies. Design Council, London

Dicks B (2014) Action, experience, communication: three methodological paradigms for researching multimodal and multisensory settings. Qual Res 14(6):656–674

Dunne A, Raby F (2013) Speculative everything: design, fiction, and social dreaming. The MIT Press, Cambridge, MA

Howes D (2011) Chapter 9: Hearing scents, tasting sights: toward a cross-cultural multimodal theory of aesthetics. In: Bacci F, Melcher D (eds) Art and the senses. Oxford University Press, Oxford

Jewitt C (2014) Handbook of multimodal analysis. Routledge, London

Jewitt C (2017) Towards a multimodal social semiotic agenda for touch. In: Zhao S, Djonov E, Bjorkvall A, Boerils M (eds) Advancing multimodal and critical discourse studies: interdisciplinary research. Routledge, London, pp 79–93

Jewitt C, Leder Mackley K (2018) Methodological dialogues across multimodality and sensory ethnography: digital touch communication. Qual Res 19(1):90–110

Jewitt C, Price S (2019) Family touch practices and learning experiences in the museum. Sens Soc J 14(2):221–235

Jewitt C, Bezemer J, O'Halloran K (2016) Introducing multimodality. Routledge, London

Jewitt C, Xambo A, Price S (2017) Exploring methodological innovation in the social sciences: the body in digital environments and the arts. Int J Soc Res Method 20(1):105–120

Jewitt C, Leder Mackley K, Atkinson D, Price S (2019) Rapid prototyping for social science research. In: Pauwels L, Mannay D (eds) The SAGE handbook of visual research methods, 2nd edn. Sage, London. (in press)

Kress G (2010) Multimodality: exploring contemporary methods of communication. Routledge, London

Kress G, Jewitt C, Bourne J, Franks A, Hardcastle J, Jones K (2005) Urban English classrooms: multimodal perspectives. Routledge, London

Kress G, Jewitt C, Ogborn J (2014) Multimodal teaching and learning. Continuum/Bloomsbury, London

Leder Mackley K, Pink S (2013) From emplaced knowing to interdisciplinary knowledge: sensory ethnography in energy research. Sens Soc 8:335–353

Leder Mackley K, Pink S (2014) Framing and educating attention: a sensory apprenticeship in the context of domestic energy research. In: Arantes L, Rieger E (eds) Ethnographien der Sinne: Wahrnehmung und Methode in empirisch-kulturwissenschaftlichen Forschungen. Transcript, Bielefeld, pp 93–109

Lupton D (2018) Towards design sociology. Sociol Compass

Myers N, Dumit J (2011) Haptics: haptic creativity and mid-embodiments of experimental life. In: Mascia- Lees F (ed) A companion to the anthropology of the body and embodiment. Blackwell, London, pp 240–261

Pink S (2015) Doing sensory ethnography, 2nd edn. Sage, London

Price S, Jewitt C, Sakr M (2016) Embodied experiences of place: a study of history learning with mobile technologies. J Comput Assist Learn 32(4):345–359

Rogers Y, Yuill N, Marshall P (2013) Contrasting lab-based and in-the-wild studies for evaluating multi-user technologies. In: Price S, Jewitt C, Brown B (eds) The SAGE handbook of digital technology research. Sage, London

Salazar J, Pink S, Irving A, eds SJ (2017) Anthropologies and futures: researching emerging and uncertain world. Bloomsbury Academic, London

Tarr JS, Gonzalez-Polledo EJ, Cornish F (2017) On liveness: using arts workshops as a research method. Qual Res 18(1):36–52

Zhang EY, Cheok AD (2016) Forming intimate human-robot relationships through a kissing machine. In: Proceedings of the fourth international conference on human agent interaction (HAI '16), New York, NY, USA

Chapter 3
The Terrain of Digital Touch Communication

Abstract This chapter provides a descriptive map of digitally mediated touch communication. Whilst acknowledging our everyday interaction with touch screens, our focus is on emergent and semi-speculative touch technologies that want us to be able to touch and feel objects in new ways: from tangibles, wearables, haptics for virtual reality, through to the tactile internet of skin. It gives an overview of current state-of-the-art digital touch technologies, that enable new forms of touch communication in various contexts, such as work, leisure, learning, personal and social relationships and health and well-being. The chapter assess the scope, extent and findings of user studies to date, and identifies emerging issues around the social aspects of digital touch communication, that might involve human-object, human-human, human to robot or robot to human touch. In so doing, this map documents the resources for touch, the touch interactions supported and the kinds of touch communication practices that are being designed and identifies the social potentials and constraints of touch that are taken up by the designers of 'digital touch'.

Keywords Digital touch · Haptics · Technology · Contact-haptics · Non-contact haptics · Human-human touch · Robotic-touch · Virtual touch · Communication

3.1 Introduction

In Chap. 1, we made a case for the significance of touch for communication and suggested that developments in sensory digital technologies are bringing touch to the fore in ways that move digital communication beyond 'ways of seeing' to include new 'ways of feeling'. We argued that this shift requires us to take new measure of digitally mediated touch, or 'digital touch', as a communicational resource, what it is and can be, how it is designed and imagined, and its communicative potentials and limitations.

C. Jewitt et al., *Interdisciplinary Insights for Digital Touch Communication*, Human–Computer Interaction Series,
https://doi.org/10.1007/978-3-030-24564-1_3

In this chapter we build on this argument to map the current state-of-the-art digital touch technologies through an extensive review of the literature. We look beyond our everyday interaction with touch screens, to focus on emergent and semi-speculative touch technologies that 'want us' and 'make' us want to be able to touch and feel objects in new ways: from tangibles, wearables, haptics for virtual reality, through to the tactile internet of skin. We begin to map the complex terrain of digital touch by drawing attention to key developments in digital touch capacity; specifically contact and non-contact haptics. We then map the array of digital touch communication research in relation to different communicative relationships: human-human touch, human-robot/robot-human touch, and human-object touch. We use these conceptual distinctions to help to raise questions and start debates about the interlinked nature of social issues that arise across these different communication spaces and contexts, whilst acknowledging that there is inevitably some overlap of the technologies/devices being developed and designed for use across these different contexts. Finally, the chapter, provides an overview of the scope, extent and findings of user studies to date, and in so doing, starts to document the resources for touch, the touch interactions supported and the kinds of touch communication practices that are being designed and starts to bring to the surface the social potentials and constraints of touch that are taken up by the designers of digital touch.

Primarily technologies being developed for digital touch communication involve some form of 'haptics'. Haptics investigates "human-machine communication through the sense of touch in interactions where we can not only use our sense of touch for input, but also receive computer generated touch output." (Huisman 2017, p. 391). Haptic technologies are used to convey human touch sensations (contact location, pressure, slip, vibration, temperature) and kinaesthetic perception (position, orientation, force). To do this, engineers and computer scientists need to measure human movement and sensations and match these to 'haptic' sensations that can be generated by various means and provided to the user. Haptic technologies can simulate various physical properties, such as the weight of an object, the feeling of friction, texture or resistance, or temperature.

There are two forms of haptic technologies: contact and non-contact. Contact haptics use specific input and output devices, such as data gloves or joysticks, for users to feel different, often mechanically generated, sensations, through force feedback or vibrating sensors (Smith and MacLean 2007; Bailenson et al. 2007; Takahashi et al. 2011), which can also be embedded into textiles and wearable devices. Responding to the importance of touch for human development and well-being, and recent empirical work suggesting that conveying emotion is possible through tactile interfaces that enable haptic communication between people (e.g. Réhman and Li 2010), a large tranche of research is taking place in the field of 'affective haptics' for interpersonal communication. Contact haptics are increasing the potential to generate physical sensations across a distance, e.g. using vibration, force feedback or mechanical motors integrated into various devices or materials, including wearable technologies. In so doing, this is changing the role of touch in communication – which is typically thought of as being co-located, with skin on skin, or skin on object – by extending the potential to use the 'touch' channel of communication remotely. Huisman (2017) offers a comprehensive review of haptic technology for social touch. Simulating touch is becoming an increasingly important consideration in virtual reality contexts, for enhancing feelings of immersion and fostering natural interactions through improving multisensory feedback, and for gestural interaction. A variety of approaches are being explored from haptic 'digits' (e.g. GoTouch VR) to haptic gloves (e.g. HaptX), combining touch feedback with touchless gestural interaction. HaptX gloves use microfluidics to create sensations of rigidity and softness through inflation creating indents into the skin to mimic skin depressions that result from holding or pressing physical objects in the world (https://www.youtube.com/watch?v=s-HAsxt9pV4). The potential applications for this 'virtual' touch are many including telerobotics, medical or military training, manufacturing design spaces, as well as entertainment and gaming.

Non-contact haptics involve the generation of physical touch sensations, or haptic feedback, without touching a physical object or device. Reverse electro-vibration is an augmented reality (AR) technology that generates a weak electric field around the user's skin, allowing users to perceive the textures and contours of remote objects, without the use of gloves or specialised devices. Mid-air haptics (also called touch-less gesture tracking devices) uses ultrasound to make air pressure changes around the user's hand, generating a physical sensation on the hand in mid-air, and usually combined with visual and/or auditory feedback. User studies suggest effective use in AR (Dzidek et al. 2018) their potential for use in VR/AR, music, robotics, automotive and teleoperation (Giordano et al. 2018).

Beyond haptics, advances in biosensing technologies, can generate information about the physical state of another, or of oneself, or embedded sensors can provide physical sensing of the wider environment. These technologies generate new ways to capture the quality of touch, or the environment that differently mediates touch interaction, and may even alter the very notion and possibilities of touch. For example, the Spanish avant-garde artist and cyborg activist Moon Ribas' implanted a vibrating sensor in her arm, to detect real-time seismic activity from around the world. In relation to the Nepal earthquake she says, "It felt very weird, like I was there," she says. "I feel connected to the people who suffer through an earthquake." (Quito 2016).

In the context of robotics, developments predominantly focus on the hands for touching, with two different approaches. One is to develop just the necessary digits or qualities for the robot to perform a task it is designed for: this might mean only 2 or 3 finger grippers – a typical design for robots doing factory line picking and moving. The other approach is to develop robot hands as close to the human hand as possible, both in structure and function (e.g. Bianchi and Moscatelli 2016; Xu and Todorov 2016). However, much of this work concerns dexterity and movement, which although critical, are not so directly related to 'touch'. Research on touch in robotics seeks to understand discrimination of the touch senses, both for humans and technically. For robots, the need to discriminate the meaning of a specific touch e.g. in sports or yoga, where tactile moving of a person's body helps to gain the correct posture (DallaLibera et al. 2011), and the sensitivity of their touch movements is clearly important. Substantial progress has been made in the development of dexterity and sensitivity of robotic hands, in terms of their ability to detect objects and adjust, for example, the pressure with which to hold an object. Güler et al. (2014)

explored how effectively robots can recognise substances by 'feeling' or 'squeezing', in comparison with using vision and touch, just vision or just touch. Findings suggest that vision alone and touch alone are similar in accuracy, and this improves when using both vision and touch. Alternatively, GelSight sensors (e.g. GelSight 2017) can be attached to robotic arms. These consist of transparent rubber, coated on one side with reflective metallic paint, that takes on the shape of an object when the surface is pressed against it. Current findings from both approaches suggest key effective features are rigidity or hardness, but more sensitivity is needed using, for example, vibration with tap or shake movements.

More extensively touch related, are skin-like technologies, where engineers and computer scientists aim to develop multisensorial material to cover large areas – similar to human skin – with a view to improving autonomous robots and enhancing biomimetic prosthetics, for example, Skinware (Youssefi et al. 2015) (foundation for Cyskin), e-skin (Hammock et al. 2013), iSkin (Coclite, Smart Artifical Skin, Weigel et al. 2015). E-skin comprises multimodal sensor skins that may be useful in: allowing robots to better sense their direct environment; soft prostheses that are capable of sensing contact, pressure or temperature; and as health-monitoring devices (Windmiller and Wang 2013). Hammock et al. (2013) place the start of e-skin to a 1974 prosthetic hand with discrete sensor feedback. E-skin then evolved to touch screens (1984, Hewlett Packard) to a material sensitive skin enabling a robotic arm to sense obstacles and avoid them (General Electric, 1985), to the 1990s when flexible electronic materials with large areas of force sensors were developed. In the early 2000s there was a rapid increase in the development of the integration of a wider array of sensors, using flexible, stretchable high-performance sensing capabilities, which aim to mimic human skin more closely, (e.g. Sekitani et al. 2014).

Drawing on these developments, iSkin integrates capacitive and resistive touch sensors that sense two levels of pressure, whether stretched or not, and supports multi and single touch (Weigel et al. 2015). It is flexible and stretchable and able to fit any area of the body, providing the opportunity for new types of on body devices, including finger-worn devices and extensions to conventional wearable devices. Studies of touch sensor recognition when worn in different areas of the body (the forearm, back of the hand and index finger) show high accuracy but identified challenges of low spatial resolution, issues of continuous pressure, and avoiding unintentional touch events. While e-skin technologies are progressing, this field of research is in its infancy, and few user studies or implementation of the technology 'in the wild' have been undertaken.

3.2 Human-Human Digitally Mediated Touch Communication

Globalisation, migration and changes in labour have led an increased need for communication at a distance, highlighting the changing place of touch in human to human communication. Enhanced portability and connectivity of the digital, has provided extensive changes to remote communication through video links, but more recent technical developments, bring new opportunities for new digitally mediated forms of social touch.

Much work in this area focuses on conveying or communicating emotion. Force feedback and vibrating sensors have been shown to be successful in conveying emotions, including angry, delighted, relaxed and happy (Smith and MacLean 2007, Bailenson et al. 2007). Other work shows how emotional experiences (e.g. hilarity) can be shared at a distance, through vibration triggered by either party watching the same movie (Takahashi et al. 2011). However, higher feelings of connectedness were found when combining speech and touch in a story telling scenario, using an upper arm touch device linked to a pressure sensitive casing on a mobile phone (Wang et al. 2012). These selected examples illustrate that force feedback or vibration can play a role in supporting mediated social or affective touch, specifically in terms of feelings of connectedness.

Textile sensors or wearable devices can also heighten and extend touch to communicate connection across distance, e.g. Ring∗U, a touch ring that provides vibrotactile feedback through an embedded eccentric mass vibration motor to 'hug' the wearer's finger (Choi et al. 2014), or through stroking someone wearing digitally augmented clothing (Seeley 2011), or new ways of sensing the intention of, e.g. soft, touch from the way the hands move or the muscle activates through electromyography (Schirmer et al. 2011). A number of haptic jackets embedded with actuators enhance immersion in gaming or movie watching (e.g. Emojacket, Arafsha et al. 2012), and immersion in sports. For example, the 'hugshirt' or the 'alert shirt' (from We:eX) enable football fans to 'feel' what the players are feeling, e.g. heart rate changes or bump from a collision between players, through haptic feedback on the t-shirt. Here we see an example of how similar technologies are used for both individual 'information' or experience, and for connecting people.

An alternative focus has been on how technology might be exploited to realise the sense of physical/emotional warmth (Willemse 2015). For example 'The Hug' (DiSalvo et al. 2003), is an anthropomorphic cushion that communicates hugs by means of vibro-tactile and warm thermal feedback, 'YourGloves', 'HotHands', and 'HotMits' (Gooch and Watts 2010), support the feeling of holding hands over a distance, and 'Huggy Pajama' (Teh et al. 2008), reproduce hugs by means of inflatable air pockets and heating elements. This kind of warmth has been shown to enhance the idea of presence of 'another' (Gooch and Watts 2010).

While the field of affective haptics has shown how emergent technologies can differently connect people through touch sensations, and can be effective in achieving "a higher level of emotional immersion during media consumption, … communicating valence and arousal, and the emotions of happiness, sadness, anger and fear" (Eid and Osman 2016: 1), a number of challenges are also raised. The contextual impact of human interpretation of haptic communication is significant (Eid and Osman 2016), especially since mediated touch is dependent on the particular relationship between communicators, where in intimate situations touch can be seen as appropriate, but can generate discomfort in strangers (e.g. Smith and MacLean 2007; Rantala et al. 2013). The need for more insights into the effects of temperature-based stimuli and the role of other modalities in conjunction with the 'touch' itself is essential (Willemse et al. 2015), as well as the type of feedback that is most successful for conveying different emotions in different contexts e.g. warmth to reduce stress, haptic for social interaction (Huisman 2017). This is particularly important since attribution seems to form a large part of the mediated touch experience – where the haptic feedback need not necessarily feel 'real' but is attributed to the sender – another person or social actor – and thus takes on social significance (Huisman 2017).

We can see that various characteristics of touch form the basis of empirical research studies, such as: physical warmth (Willemse et al. 2015); notions of connectedness (Wang et al. 2012); different textures and wearables (Ebe and Umemuro 2015); developing meaning and ludic experience through conveying messages in gaming (Canat et al. 2016); or conveying different emotional feelings (Huisman 2017).

3.3 Human-Robot and Robot-Human Touch

Robots can be designed to look like humans, but the majority take other physical forms, the key factor being that they are programmed to automatically carry out a complex series of actions or tasks. While some robot designs include haptic sensors to provide the capacity for touch sensing, their automatic actions take them beyond 'haptic devices' per se. Nevertheless, touch is an important component in various areas of robotics research including affective and social contexts, and teleoperations.

3.3.1 Affective and Social Robot Touch

Since the 2000s, due to converging advances in technology and the changing social and economic landscapes of health, care and work, interest in 'affective and social touch' in robot-human and human-robot touch communication has grown. There are a number of research perspectives, including: research that seeks to understand human perceptions of robots, since this will impact the degree to which they are likely to be effective in affective or social communication; research which focuses on the mechanisms by which robot touch communication can elicit affective responses in humans; and the development and (sometimes) evaluation of robotic devices for promoting affective communication with humans. Some researchers classify interactions according to robot-initiated, human initiated or cooperative touch (Chen et al. 2011). In robot initiated touch the robot initiates contact with the human e.g. in care contexts (Mukai et al. 2010), in human initiated touch the human makes physical contact with the robot first e.g. with robot 'pets' (Yohanan and MacLean 2009), and in cooperative touch both are actively engaged in contact e.g. shaking hands (Shiomi et al. 2007). For technically mediated touch between robot and human, it is important to sensitively consider two key affective aspects of robotic interpersonal communication: being able to both convey emotion or meaning through touch, as well as interpret emotion or meaning through touch, as well as physical aspects, such as degree of pressure being exerted.

Given the importance of touch in social development and communication, there are assumed benefits for developing affective touch interaction between robotic agents and humans, requiring robot-initiated touch research. For example, Furuhashi et al. (2015) developed a robot that alerts the human of, for example, an incoming telephone call. When a call comes in the robot actively touches the person to alert them. User studies with adults showed challenges for the robot in negotiating obstacles in the room, detecting the location of, and recognising, the human.

For many researchers, the bi-directional connection between robots and humans is key. Rather than focusing on initiation of contact, work in this area includes developing prototype devices to explore the contact-expressive ability of the technology, while others engage more deeply in understanding human emotion and translating these characteristics in ways that can be emulated in robots. Erp and Toet (2015) argue that empathic communication is critical for social agents to improve social relations, and that social agents/robots with touch capabilities elicit more empathy and motivation to engage from humans e.g. in simulation, virtual patients able to touch back were treated more like humans than when not.

Affective touch prototypes have been developed to explore both human perception of affect and affective engagement with the robot device, and the effectiveness of the various haptic designs in conveying emotion. For example, pillows that respond to different kinds of stroking, pressure, and heat, or blankets embedded with electronics and computation, and which move and physically interact with people (e.g. Linköping 2004). However, no studies with these have been reported. In terms of robotic-touch and well-being, studies suggest benefits of pet robots in reducing stress and depression (Yohanan and MacLean 2011; Takayanagi et al. 2014), some of which specifically identify the role of touch – stroking, petting and hugging – in reducing systolic and diastolic blood pressure (Robinson et al. 2015) and mimicking hand massage experiences, which have been shown to release stress-relieving hormones (Remington 2002).

Research has shown that understanding human perceptions of robot communication is also critical in designing robots (Chen et al. 2011; Wullenkord et al. 2016). Motivated by the desire for robots to be as human-like as possible, Nie et al. (2012) investigated whether the temperature of a robot's hand influences perception of the robot's emotional warmth. Findings of a study with 39 participants suggest that experiences of physical warmth increased feelings of friendship and trust, but also raised the issue of exacerbating the 'uncanny valley' problem (i.e. the phenomenon whereby a too realistic humanoid robot arouses a sense of unease or revulsion in the person viewing it), and the need to take human expectations into consideration. Orefice et al. (2016) designed a robot hand with specific pressure points based on the human handshake and showed that gender and extroversion personality traits were interpreted, on the basis of firmness and movement of the hand during shaking, highlighting the communicative/ interpretative capacity of touch. (The ways in which digital touch is gendered is explored in relation to social norms in Chap. 4.)

A complimentary focus of research explores ways in which human touch can elicit changes in robot response (Martinez-Hernandez 2016). Here a model of touch is used to control robot facial expression, with five processing layers: sensation, perception, decision, action and worlds, which allow a human to change the robot's (iCub) emotional state through tactile interaction. The researchers, experimenting with human to robot touch to assess the robot expression, found accurate recognition and response to actions like pinch/ stroke.

Longstanding ethical issues and the broadening of the ethical landscape beyond the human to include (in this case) the robot, are explored in Chap. 7.

3.3.2 Teleoperation

The field of teleoperation or telerobotics (operating a machine or robot from a distance) has a wide range of applications. Telerobots are used in the manufacturing industry for factory line picking and moving, for undertaking dangerous work, such as, bomb disposal or firefighting (Lawson et al. 2016), and in medicine, space, and marine contexts. Typically, a human operator controls a robot from a distance and receives feedback that informs whether the robot has followed instructions or completed the task.

As early as 1999 Fujita and Hashimoto demonstrated that technology can link together the actions of a robot arm remotely, so that moving the master arm will elicit the same movements in the robot arm. They also showed that users could feel their partner through force feedback, but not be able to see them. An example of training robots to recognise touch through learning from demonstration can be seen in firefighter training (Lawson et al. 2016). In this context, the robot nozzle operator needs to 'understand' human touch commands. Since force sensing resistors cannot be put all over the robot, Lawson et al., explore the use of LEAP motion sensors to recognise visual touch gestures, and use learning from demonstration (LfD) to teach the robot to recognise and react to various gestures. Similar methods are used with haptic gloves (e.g. HaptX, Shadow Robots and Syntouch), where leap motion sensors, attached to the glove, detect specific hand and digit movements and location, are used to elicit appropriate haptic feedback. However, in this case the gloves actually allow humans to sense what the robot is feeling (Aouf 2019), and are being designed for use in telerobotic contexts, such as, bomb disposal, space exploration and construction.

Another interesting area of 'touch' research concerns 'body ownership transfer' (Ogawa et al. 2012), where a teleoperator working with a robot can perceive the touch on the robot as if they themselves have been touched. In the teleoperator situation, only visual signals are received, and it is the visual event of the robot being touched that elicits the feeling of the operator being touched. Inoue et al. (2015) undertook a study with 8 adults to examine sense of body ownership, sense of agency, and mirror self-recognition ratings based on robot mobility and sensory-motor congruency, but their findings did not provide evidence for improved body ownership. In general, there seems to be little research to date that explores the concept of touch during robot training or robot manipulation e.g. understanding human perceptions of transferring their own notion of touch to that of the robot – whether it heightens awareness of the qualities of their touch, or its impact on their training or practice.

3.4 Human-Object Touch Communication

In this section, we look at how touch-based technologies (excluding robots) are enabling new communicative capacities between humans and physical or virtual objects.

3.4.1 Object/Textile Handling

With a predominance in online shopping, the textile industry is developing haptic based techniques for effectively conveying tactile qualities of materials (Perry et al. 2013). Touch is critical for customers and designers, who select clothing not only on the basis of what it looks like, but also how it feels, how the material falls and moves around the body. One approach to simulate or mimic texture and tactile elements of materials is to augment touch-like gestures e.g. a pinch gesture would lead to the material being visually scrunched (Orzechowski et al. 2011). Shoogleit, an application based on this idea, it was trialled with 218 university students (mostly female), who explored a chiffon dress or a man's cotton shirt using the rotate (finger used to rotate the garment) and scrunch (pinch with visual image) capabilities (Cano et al. 2017), showed that the visual and touch were equal in their effect. Another approach is through 'haptography' (Culbertson et al. 2018), a combination of haptics and photography, where a stylus haptic device records textural data from different materials. This data is translated into various forms of haptic feedback, that enables different surfaces to be 'felt' through the stylus e.g. silk or canvas, although no user studies outside of the engineering lab are evident.

Other haptic technologies offer new opportunities for 3D object handling. ProbosVR, a tool akin to the phantom, uses a 3D interactive system that enables museum visitors to interact with scanned replicas of objects through 'touching' the objects using a joystick-like stylus, linked to related images, audio and video on an adjacent screen. Alternatively, devices like the vibrotactile glove enables users to feel 3D virtual objects in conjunction with seeing them (e.g. Martínez et al. 2016). Using a different technology – ultrahaptics – users can experience similar tactile interaction with visually projected (rather than physical) objects (e.g. Carter et al. 2013), where different textured surfaces can be recognised (Freeman et al. 2017).

Given the predominance of touch screens, electrovibration, a relatively new approach in the field of haptics, enables new user experiences that bring improved and increased kinds of touch experiences to 'flat' visualisations.

Reverse electro-vibration enables physical objects to be augmented with different textures, creating artificial tactile sensations to almost any surface or object (REVEL, Bau et al. 2010). Typically, the research to date is taking place in museums, as well as entertainment and gaming contexts.

3.4.2 *Education and Training*

Research around touch and haptic technologies in education is somewhat disparate in terms of devices or systems, and topics or learning contexts. With children it has typically focused on those with tactile sensory loss or visual impairment, for rehabilitation purposes, or navigation (Patomäki et al. 2004). Research with mainstream learners has primarily focused on high school science, using the omni Phantom or joysticks, for example: sensing resistance between two molecules; simple machines (levers, gears, pulleys etc.); experiencing magnetic forces, mechanical forces; and for exploring viruses and nanoscale science; (ibid, pp. 2283). In mathematics the omni Phantom has been used to support dynamic geometry learning for 10 year olds (haptic with 3D visuals) (Güçler et al. 2013), trigonometry, using multimodal dynamic representations (abstract, visual and haptic) attaching haptic feedback to sine waves (Davis et al. 2017), and primary school geometry learning (Yiannoutsou, Johnson and Price 2018). With adults, the vibro-tactile glove has been explored to provide a haptic sensation of tracing the borders of 3D objects, but studies suggest that long training times are needed to develop the ability to perceive shapes (Martínez et al. 2016).

While research into the use of haptic technologies for school education is in its infancy, medical education and clinical contexts have adopted various 'touch' related technologies for enabling student practice of medical procedures, e.g. surgical, dental, and for improving efficiency and patient safety in surgical practice itself. For example, in dentistry, a stylus device can be used to feel over teeth to detect soft and hard surfaces of teeth to assess whether they need filling (Kuchenbecker et al. 2017). HAPtel extends this idea, using virtual reality in conjunction with the physical phantom device that represents a dental tool, to enable dental students to interact with a 3D mouth space to feel the different layers of a tooth when drilling (e.g. San Diego et al. 2012). Successful evaluation has led to extending this experience to practical restorative procedures. Haptics is also thought to be valuable in both practicing and undertaking minimally invasive surgical procedures, where the surgeon is separated from the patient and uses a robotic arm to do the operation. For example, work in the Haptic Intelligence Lab is exploring how to implement tactile feedback through instrument vibrations to reintroduce a sense of touch into procedures where touch is critical to the manipulations and actions being performed (e.g. Brown et al. 2017).

3.4.3 *Disability and Rehabilitation*

For some people living with a range of disabilities, digital touch capacities can enhance their quality of life, for example, through new rehabilitation systems, tactile applications for the blind, and e-skin for prosthetic purposes.

The tactile sense can sometimes be seen as a substitute for other sensory inputs, particularly for the visually impaired. While developing techniques that exploit the tactile sense for the visually impaired is not new (e.g. Braille Warren 1978; tactile maps or graphics, Sheppard and Aldrich 2000), developments in haptics and touch screen interfaces offer alternative ways of exploiting the tactile sense for this group, particularly for navigation, access to information and spatial awareness.

Although technologies initially used sonic feedback to facilitate mobility and navigation (e.g. Heyes 1983, miniguide), tactile stimulators provide vibration or tapping to guide the person (Ross and Blasch 2000), and the PHANToM can provide spatial information in a virtual environment (e.g. Magnusson et al. 2002). More recently the PHANToM has been used in classroom settings in the form of multimodal games for supporting visually impaired children's engagement with 3D objects tracing pathways/shapes (Patomäki et al. 2004), learning geometry (Yiannoutsou et al. 2018) and learning of electric circuits (Pietrzak et al. 2007).

Combined with touch screen interfaces work has focused on kinetic tactile displays which enable 'active touch' i.e. feedback coupled with location. Several of these interfaces use actuators, motors and pressure (e.g. Velazquez et al. 2008). However, these methods have disadvantages in terms of resolution and range, and cost. In contrast, TelsaTouch uses a conductive layer to provide tactile sensation to moving fingers on touch screens (Xu et al. 2011). Findings from application studies showed that difficulties with navigation need further work, the subtlety of dots in Braille was hard to perceive, but solid shapes were easier to recognise. Since the information processing capabilities of the tactile sense are lower than vision, haptic alone has been shown not to always be sufficient (Levesque 2005), leading designs to augment tactile displays with audio e.g. Talking Tactile Tablet (Wells and Landau 2003), or thermal screen, with varied temperature generated by the embedded LED bulbs, that allows a blind person to paint colourful pictures on the tablet (Kos et al. 2016).

Moving away from screens, haptics in the form of clothing and textiles, vibrotactile gloves, VR and e-skin devices are being researched for rehabilitation purposes. Clothing and textiles designed to convey information about the wearer can be used for navigation, e.g. through vibration in shoes (Rowley 2016) or to correct posture through directional feedback in clothing indicating which way to rotate e.g. the ankle, with frequency and vibration being used to convey how far off the correct position the wearer is (Van Dongen 2017).

Interactive experiences that aim to foster rehabilitation are being developed in VR, using controllers or vibrotactile gloves. A review (Rose et al. 2018) of 18 papers to explore research findings related to enjoyment, rehabilitation routine and health outcomes, and the role of haptic feedback on VR immersion and performance, showed that haptic controllers served to increase movement accuracy, while gloves decreased movement velocity. Use of the vibrotactile glove has shown slight improvements in muscle strength and hand movement for post stroke patients (Hsiao-Ching et al. 2017). A review of VR (joysticks, Kinect, but not headsets) for rehabilitation for children with cerebral palsy, shows improvement in balance and motor skills (alongside traditional rehabilitation methods) (Ravi et al. 2017).

More recently, an e-skin sensing device with a view to use in prosthetics, was developed using electrotactile stimulation. Testing with 8 healthy participants, to see if they could recognise shape, position and direction of mechanical stimuli presented on e-skin, showed good performance levels, but highlighted challenges of computational complexity in successfully integrating e-skin into prosthetic devices (Franceschi et al. 2016).

From this overview, we can see an increasing number of contexts and applications are employing haptic or sensor technologies to convey information to users in different social and communication contexts, including object or textile handling in museums and commerce, education and medical training, and to alleviate issues of disability, through rehabilitation, prosthetics or enhanced forms of interaction.

3.5 Conclusion

This chapter has provided a foray into the landscape of digital touch technologies. Technological development in this area is somewhat in its infancy but it is bringing a diverse set of techniques and engineering capacities, as well as various approaches to informing or underpinning designs and applications, depending on the area of use. As we have seen, digital touch technologies are being developed for health and well-being, education, personal relationships, industry and work contexts, each demanding different consideration. While some touch (haptic) technologies have been integrated into, for example, medical training, a significant proportion are in the early stages of research development, perhaps more at a 'proof of concept' stage. This is especially true for VR (Stone 2001, 2019), but also the many challenges facing robot interaction with humans, not only with respect to human interpretation of robot intention and robot understanding and navigation, but also in terms of significant ethical issues. From the mapping of this landscape we now turn to the social and cultural questions, issues and considerations raised by digital touch.

References

Aouf RS (2019) Robot hand with sense of touch lets humans feel delicate objects remotely. Available via https://wwwdezeencom/2019/03/15/robot-hand-touch-shadow-robot-company-syntouch-haptx/. Accessed 17 Mar 2019

Arafsha F, Alam KM, Saddik AE (2012) EmoJacket: consumer centric wearable affective jacket to enhance emotional immersion. Paper presented at the international conference on innovations in information technology, April, pp 350–355

Bailenson JN, Yee N, Brave S, Merget D, Koslow D (2007) Virtual interpersonal touch: expressing and recognizing emotions through haptic devices. Hum Comput Interact 22(3):325–353

Bau O, Poupyrev I, Israr A, Harrison C (2010) TeslaTouch: electrovibration for touch surfaces. In: proceedings of UIST'10, ACM, pp 283–292

Bianchi M, Moscatelli A (2016) Human and robot hands: sensorimotor synergies to bridge the gap between neuroscience and robotics. Springer, Cham

Brown JD, Fernandez JN, Cohen SP, Kuchenbecker KJA (2017) Wrist-squeezing force-feedback system for robotic surgery training. In: Proceedings of the IEEE world haptics conference, Munich, Germany, June 2017, pp 107–112

Canat M, Tezcan MO, Yurdakull C, Tiza E, Sefercik BC, Bostan I, Buruk OT, Göksun T, Özca O (2016) Sensation: measuring the effects of a human-to-human social touch based controller on the player experience. In: Proceedings of CHI'16, May 07–12, San Jose, CA, USA

Cano MB, Perry P, Ashman R, Waite K (2017) The influence of image interactivity upon user engagement when using mobile touch screens. Comput Hum Behav 77:406–412

Carter T, Seah SA, Long B, Drinkwater B, Subramanian S (2013) UltraHaptics: multi-point mid-air haptic feedback for touch surfaces. In: Proceedings of the 26th symposium on user interface software and technology, UIST '13. ACM Press, New York, pp 505–514

Chen T, King C, Thomaz A, Kemp C (2011) Touched by a robot: an investigation of subjective responses to robot-initiated touch. In: Proceedings of the 6th ACM/IEEE international conference on human-robot interaction, pp 457–464

Choi Y, Tewell J, Morisawa Y, Pradana GA, Cheok A (2014) Ring∗U: a wearable system for intimate communication using tactile lighting expressions. In: Proceedings of the 11th conference on advances in computer entertainment technology, Article No. 63

Culbertson H, Schorr SB, Okamura AM (2018) Haptics: the present and future of artificial touch sensation. Annu Rev Control Robot Auton Syst 1(1):385–409

DallaLibera F, Basoeki F, Minato T, Ishiguro H, Menegatti E (2011) Teaching by touching: interpretation of tactile instructions for motion development. In: IEEE/RSJ international conference on intelligent robots and systems, pp 3480–3487

Davis RL, Orta Martinez M, Schneider O, MacLean KE, Okamura AM, Blikstein P (2017) The haptic bridge: towards a theory for haptic-supported learning. In: Proceedings of the 18th conference on interaction design and children. ACM Press, New York, pp 51–60

DiSalvo C, Gemperle F, Forlizzi J, Montgomery E (2003) The hug: an exploration of robotic form for intimate communication. In: Proceedings of 12th IEEE international workshop on robot and human interactive communication, pp 403–408

Dzidek B, Frier W, Harwood A, Hayden R (2018) Design and evaluation of mid-air haptic interactions in an augmented reality environment. In: Prattichizzo D, Shinoda H, Tan H, Ruffaldi E, Frisoli A (eds) Haptics: science, technology, and applications. EuroHaptics 2018. Lecture notes in computer science. Springer, Cham, p 10894

Ebe Y, Umemuro H (2015) Emotion evoked by texture and application to emotional communication. In: Proceedings of 33rd annual conference extended abstracts on human factors in computing systems ACM, New York, USA 1995–2000

Eid MA, Osman HA (2016) Affective haptics: current research and future directions. IEEE Access 4:26–40

Erp JBFV, Toet A (2015) Social touch in human computer interaction. Frontiers in Digital Humanities 27th May 2015

Franceschi M, Seminara L, Pinna L, Valle M, Ibrahim A, Dosen S (2016) Towards the integration of e-skin into prosthetic devices. In: Proceedings of 12th conference on Ph.D. research in microelectronics and electronics, pp 1–4

Freeman E, Anderson R, Williamson J, Wilson G, Brewster S (2017) Textured surfaces for ultrasound haptic displays. In: Proceedings of 19th ACM international conference on multimodal interaction, Glasgow, UK, November 13–17

Furuhashi M, Nakamura T, Kanoh M, Yamada K (2015) Touch-based information transfer from a robot modeled on the hearing dog. In: International conference on fuzzy systems 1–6, IEEE

GelSight (2017). Available at: https://eandt.theiet.org/content/articles/2017/06/tactile-sensors-give-robot-pincers-greater-dexterity-and-sensitivity/. Accessed 19 June 2019

Giordano M, Georgiou O, Dzidek B, Corenthy L, Kim JR, Subramanian S, Brewster A (2018) Mid-air haptics for control interfaces. In: Extended abstracts CHI conference on human factors in computing systems. ACM, New York

Gooch D, Watts LA (2010) YourGloves, hothands and hotmits: devices to hold hands at a distance. In: Proceedings of the 25th annual ACM symposium on user interface software and technology, pp 157–166

Güçler B, Hegedus S, Robidoux R, Jackiw N (2013) Investigating the mathematical discourse of young learners involved in multi-modal mathematical investigations: the case of haptic technologies. In: Martinovic D, Freiman V, Karadag Z (eds) Visual mathematics and cyberlearning, vol 1. Springer, Dordrecht, pp 97–118

Güler P, Bekiroglu Y, Gratal X, Pauwels K, Kragic D (2014) What's in the container? Classifying object contents from vision and touch. In: International conference on intelligent robots and systems IEEE, pp 3961–3968

Hammock ML, Chortos A, Tee BCK, Tok JBH, Bao Z (2013) 25th anniversary article: the evolution of electronic skin (E-skin): a brief history, design considerations, and recent Progress. Adv Mater 25(42):5997–6038

Heyes T (1983) Human navigation by sound. Phys Technol 14:68–75

Hsiao-Ching W, Yi-Chinga L, Ya-Hsinga C, Pei-Chengb S, Chia-Minc T, Chi-Ying L (2017) The potential effect of a vibrotactile glove rehabilitation system on motor recovery in chronic post-stroke hemiparesis. Technol Health Care 25(6):1183–1187

Huisman G (2017) Social touch technology: a survey of haptic technology for social touch. IEEE Trans Haptics 99:1–1

Inoue S, Makino Y, Shinoda H (2015) Active touch perception produced by airborne ultrasonic haptic hologram. In: World haptics conference IEEE, pp 362–367

Kos A, Boron K, Ireneusz B (2016) Thermal tablet for the blind. Microelectron Int Bradford 33(1):1–8

Kuchenbecker KJ, Parajon R, Maggio MP (2017) Evaluation of a vibrotactile simulator for dental caries detection. Simul Healthc 12(3):148–156

Lawson W, Sullivan K, Narber C, Bekele E, Hiatt LM (2016) Touch recognition and learning from demonstration (LfD) for collaborative human-robot firefighting teams. In: 25th IEEE international symposium on robot and human interactive communication, pp 994–999

Levesque V (2005) Blindness, technology and haptics. Report number: CIM-TR-05.08, Affiliation: Centre for Intelligent Machines, McGill University

Linköping KM (2004) A touch of the future: contact-expressive devices. Media impact. IEEE Computer Society

Magnusson C, Rassmus-Gröhn K, Sjöström C, Danielsson H (2002) Navigation and recognition in complex haptic virtual environments reports from an extensive study with blind users. In: Eurohaptics 2002, Edinburgh, UK, July 2002

Martinez Hernandez U (2016) Tactile Sensors. In: Prescott TJ, Ahissar E, Izhikevich E (eds) Scholarpedia of touch. Springer, pp 783–796

Martínez J, García A, Oliver M, Molina JP, González P (2016) Identifying virtual 3D geometric shapes with a vibrotactile glove. IEEE Comput Graph Appl 36(1):42–51

Mukai T, Hirano S, Nakashima H, Kato,Y, Sakaida Y, Guo S, Hosoe S (2010) Development of a nursing-care assistant robot RIBA that can lift a human in its arms. In: IEE/RSJ international conference on intelligent robots and systems, pp 5996–6001

Nie J, Park M, Marin AL, Sundar SS (2012) Can you hold my hand? Physical warmth in human-robot interaction. In: Proceedings of 7th ACM/IEEE international conference on human-robot interaction, vol 201, p 202

Ogawa K, Taura K, Nishio S, Ishiguro H (2012) Effect of perspective change in body ownership transfer to teleoperated android robot. In: Proceedings of 21st IEEE international symposium on robot and human interactive communication, pp 1072–1077

Orefice PH, Ammi M, Hafez M, Tapus A (2016) Let's handshake and I'll know who you are: gender and personality discrimination in human-human and human-robot handshaking interaction. In: 2016 IEEE-RAS 16th international conference on humanoid robots (Humanoids), pp 958–965

Orzechowski PM, Atkinson D, Padilla S, Methven TS, Baurley S, Chantler M (2011) Interactivity to enhance perception: does increased interactivity in mobile visual presentation tools facilitate more accurate rating of textile properties? In: Proceedings of the 13th international conference on human computer interaction with mobile devices and services. ACM, New York

Patomäki S, Raisamo R, Salo J, Pasto V, Hippula A (2004) Experiences on haptic interfaces for visually impaired young children. In: Proceedings of the 6th international conference on multimodal interfaces. ACM, New York, pp 281–288

Perry P, Blazquez M, Padilla S (2013) Translating the need for touch to online fashion shopping via digital technology. In: Proceedings of the first international conference on digital technologies for the textile industries. University of Manchester, September 5–6

Pietrzak T, Martin B, Pecci I, Saarinen R, Raisamo R, Järvi J (2007) The micole architecture: multimodal support for inclusion of visually impaired children. In: Proceedings of the 9th international conference on multimodal interfaces. ACM, New York, pp 193–200

Quito A (2016). Available at: https://qz.com/677218/this-woman-a-self-described-cyborg-can-sense-every-earthquake-in-real-time/ Accessed 19 Mar 2019

Rantala J, Salminen K, Raisamo R (2013) Touch gestures in communicating emotional intention via vibrotactile stimulation. Int J Hum Comput Stud 7(6):679–690

Ravi DK, Kumar N, Singhi P (2017) Effectiveness of virtual reality rehabilitation for children and adolescents with cerebral palsy: an updated evidence-based systematic review. Physiotherapy 103(3):245–258

Réhman SLL (2010) IFeeling: Vibrotactile rendering of human emotions on Mobile phones. In: Jiang X, Ma MY, Chen CW (eds) Mobile multimedia processing: fundamentals, methods, and applications. Springer Berlin Heidelberg, Berlin, Heidelberg, pp 1–20

Remington R (2002) Calming music and hand massage with agitated elderly. Nurs Res 51:317–323

Robinson H, Macdonald B, Broadbent E (2015) Physiological effects of a companion robot on blood pressure of older people in residential care facility: a pilot study. Aust J Age 34:27–32

Rose T, Nam CS, Chen KB (2018) Immersion of virtual reality for rehabilitation – review. Appl Ergon 69:153–161

Ross D, Blasch B (2000) Wearable interfaces for orientation and wayfinding. In: Proceedings of the fourth international ACM conference on Assistive technologies, pp 193–200

Rowley MJ (2016) From yoga pants to smart shoes: the technology of touch. BBC News. Available at: http://www.bbc.co.uk/news/business-38385039. Accessed 19 June 2019

San Diego JP, Cox MJ, Quinn BFA, Newton JT, Banerjee A, Woolford M (2012) Researching haptics in higher education: the complexity of developing haptics virtual learning systems and evaluating its impact on students' learning. Comput Educ 59(1):156–166

Schirmer A, Teh K, Wang S, Vijayakumar R, Ching A, Nithianantham D, Escoffier N, Cheok A (2011) Squeeze me, but don't tease me: human and mechanical touch enhance visual attention and emotion discrimination. Soc Neurosci 6(3):219–230

Seeley A (2011). Available at: http://www.instructables.com/id/The-Touch-Glove/. Accessed 19 June 2019

Sekitani T, Kaltenbrunner M, Yokota T, Someya T (2014) Imperceptible electronic skin. SID Inf Disp 30(1):20–25

Sheppard L, Aldrich F (2000) Tactile graphics: a beginner's guide to graphics for visually impaired children. Prim Sci Rev 65:29–30

Shiomi M, Kanda T, Ishiguro H, Hagita N (2007) Interactive humanoid robots for a science museum. IEEE Intell Syst 22(2):25–32

Smith J, MacLean K (2007) Communicating emotion through a haptic link: design space and methodology. Int J Hum Comput Stud 65(4):376–387

Stone RJ (2001) Haptic feedback: a brief history from telepresence to virtual reality. In: Brewster S, Murray-Smith R (eds) Haptic human-computer interaction. Haptic HCI 2000. Lecture notes in computer science. Springer, Berlin/Heidelberg, p 2058

Stone RJ (2019) Haptics for VR – where are we.... really. Available at: https://wwwlinkedincom/pulse/haptics-vr-ar-where-we-really-bob-stone?articleId=6512601603734847488#comments-6512601603734847488&trk=public_profile_post. Accessed 19 June 2019

Takahashi K, Mitsuhashi H, Murata K, Norieda S, Watanabe K (2011) Improving shared experiences by haptic telecommunication. In: Proceedings of 2011 international conference on biometrics and Kansei engineering, pp 210–215

Takayanagi K, Kirita T, Shibata T (2014) Comparison of verbal and emotional responses of elderly people with mild/moderate dementia and those with severe dementia in responses to seal robot, PARO. Front Aging Neurosci 6:257–261

Teh JKS, Cheok AD, Peiris RL, Choi Y, Thuong V, Lai S (2008) Huggy Pajama: a mobile parent and child hugging communication system, in Proceedings of the 7th international conference on Interaction design and children, 2008, pp 250–257

van Dongen P (2017) Touch-sensitive denim jacket gives intimate back rubs. Available at: https://wwwdezeencom/2017/03/14/pauline-van-dongen-issho-smart-denim-jacket-touch-sensitive-back-rubs-sxsw/. Accessed 19 June 2019

Velazquez R, Pissaloux EE, Hafez M, Szewczyk J (2008) Tactile rendering with shape-memory-alloy pin-matrix. IEEE Trans Instrum Meas 57(5):1051–1057

Wang R, Quek F, Tatar D, Teh KS, Cheok AD (2012) Keep in touch: channel, expectation and experience. In: Proceedings of the SIGCHI conference on human factors in computing systems CHI '12. ACM, New York, pp 139–148

Warren DH (1978) Perception by the blind. Handbook of perception, Vol. X (perceptual ecology). Academic

Weigel M, Lu T, Bailly G, Oulasvirta A, Majidi C, Steimle J (2015) iSkin: flexible, stretchable and visually customizable on-body touch sensors for Mobile computing. In: Proceedings of the 33rd annual ACM conference on human factors in computing systems. ACM, New York, pp 2991–3000

Wells LR, Landau S (2003) Merging of tactile sensory input and audio data by means of the talking tactile tablet. In: Proc of EuroHaptics 2003, Dublin, Ireland

Willemse CJAM (2015) A warm touch of affect? In: International conference on affective computing and intelligent interaction, Xi'an, pp 766–771

Willemse CJAM, Heylen DKJ, Erp JBF (2015) Warmth in affective mediated interaction: exploring the effects of physical warmth on interpersonal warmth. International conference on affective computing and intelligent interaction:28–34

Windmiller JR, Wang J (2013) Wearable electrochemical sensors and biosensors: a review. Electroanalysis 25(1):29–46

Wullenkord R., Fraune MR, Eyssel F, Šabanović S (2016) Getting in touch: how imagined, actual, and physical contact affect evaluations of robots. In: 25th IEEE international symposium on robot and human interactive communication 980–985

Xu Z, Todorov E (2016) Design of a highly biomimetic anthropomorphic robotic hand towards artificial limb regeneration. In: IEEE international conference on robotics and automation, pp 3485–3492

Xu C, Israr A, Poupyrev I, Bau O, Harrison C (2011) Tactile display for the visually impaired using TeslaTouch. In: CHI '11 extended abstracts on human factors in computing systems. ACM, New York, pp 317–322

Yiannoutsou N, Johnson R, Price S (2018) Exploring how children interact with 3D shapes using haptic technologies. In: Proceedings of international conference on interaction design and children 533–538, Trondheim, June 19–22. ACM, New York

Yohanan S, MacLean KE (2009) A tool to study affective touch. In: CHI '09 extended abstracts on human factors in computing systems. ACM, New York, pp 4153–4158

Yohanan S, MacLean KE (2011) Design and assessment of the haptic Creature's affect display. In: Proceedings of the 6th international conference on human-robot interaction. ACM, New York, pp 473–480

Youssefi S, Denei S, Mastrogiovanni F, Cannata G (2015) Skinware 2.0: a real-time middleware for robot skin. SoftwareX 3-4(3–4):6–12

Links

ProbosVR Manchester Museum. http://www.museum.manchester.ac.uk/about/digitaltouchreplicas/

Chapter 4
Social Norms of Touch

Abstract This chapter discusses social norms with attention to their significance for researching and designing digital touch communication in a global world, notably gendered and cultural touch norms. It explores how social and cultural norms shape the ways that people (and machines) touch. Touch norms are shaped, regulated and enforced through social, economic, familial and legal mechanisms, they organise our experiences and expectations. Understanding of the touch norms that people, including digital touch researchers and designers, bring to their interactions with others provides a route into understanding the sociality that shapes digital touch. We discuss the significance of these given the expectations of the user, their touch repertoires, and the social cultural role that norms play in the take up and use of mediated digital touch communication devices and systems and environments. The chapter concludes that reflexive engagement with touch norms can provide insights and inspiration for thinking about, researching and designing digital touch communication, and help to address how cultural and gendered norms of touch might be engaged with, to constrain and re-produce or open-up the meaning potentials of digital touch.

Keywords Social norms · Touch · Culture · Gender · Hugging · Handshake · Body · Types of touch · Touching

4.1 Introduction

Social norms are shared patterns, rules and expectations of behaviour, routines or habits, which can also become internalized values. They are shaped, regulated and enforced through social, economic, familial and legal mechanisms (Foucault 2002; Butler 2004). Social norms are "the glue that keeps people together" (Jonsson and Lundmark 2017: 805). This sticky metaphor is often used to describe the power of

C. Jewitt et al., *Interdisciplinary Insights for Digital Touch Communication*, Human–Computer Interaction Series,
https://doi.org/10.1007/978-3-030-24564-1_4

touch in developing and maintaining relationships: touch as social "glue" (Linden 2016: 5), emphasising a common feature of touch and social norms.

There are social norms of touch in every group concerning who can legitimately touch who, where, how, and when, even if they are mostly tacit and implicit. Classen (2005: 13) suggests that we learn a 'mother touch', akin to a mother-tongue, through our enculturation: "A tactile code of communication that underpins the ways in which we engage with other people and the world". Touch is a cultural practice: living within a society requires learning its 'tactile regime'. Failure to do so can result in offense, rejection, and in extreme cases, legal action (Cranny-Francis 2011). Van Erp and Toet (2013: 782) argue that this also "holds for touch by social agents: if they don't conform to the rules and expectations of the users they may be considered as offensive and will appear like aliens".

Numerous studies examine how the rate and qualities of touch are inflected through culture, notably studies on touch between couples in cafes (Jourard 1966), train stations (Remland et al. 1995), airport restaurants and bars, and young people in queues at fast-food venues (Field 2003). This has led, originating with Hall (1966), to the conceptualising of high to low-contact cultures. There is general agreement that interpersonal touching is higher in contemporary Western societies than in Asian societies and that '[t]actile contact is generally said to be greater in Latin American and southern European than in America and Northern European Cultures (sometimes labelled 'non-contact' cultures)" (Finnegan 2014: 206). Such 'broad-brush comparisons' need to be treated with caution to avoid cultural over-generalisation and crude stereotyping, as touch is more varied in practice. Despite these caveats, culture is an essential aspect of how we conceive, negotiate and perform 'our sense of self' (Chung 2019: 383), and touch is a part of this process.

The integral relationship between touch, body and interaction positions gender as a significant concept with which to explore touch, and vice versa. Gender, like culture, is a complex concept, a topic of considerable debate and contested theorisation within the social sciences (Butler 2004) and HCI (Rode 2011). We approach gender as a fluid concept, recognising that both femininity and masculinity are socially constructed and undergo continual, albeit subtle, redefinition and re-inscription over time. People's lived experiences of gender, notably Trans, Intersex, Queer, and Gender-Fluid or Non-binary people (Halberstam 2018), "make visible what culture has made invisible the accomplishment of gender" (West and Zimmerman 1987: 131), and problematize a binary biological conceptualisation of gender and the derived associations of masculinity and femininity. Social norms relating to gender and sexuality influence how and who we touch. Touch is continually brought into the work of 'doing' gender, including the display of gender through notions of 'feminine' and 'masculine' touch (Goffman 1979). Classen's exploration of the links between femininity and tactility (2005: 203) leads her to highlight the "tactile intimacies and intricacies…of women's work" and the notion of "a woman's touch", behind which she suggests "lies the concept of woman *as* touch": declaring that, while men are inherently rational, women are "all body, all feeling".

4.2 Technology and Changing Social Norms

While the power of social norms creates a sense of them being monolithic and stable, social norms operate across different levels, at the level of society, at a cultural and generational level – they have long histories and strong roots, and are lived through individual practices. Social norms are in a state of continual flux, tension and negotiation pulled across these sites of life, they are (simultaneously) fluid and fixed. Their need to be constantly reproduced makes them powerful, yet vulnerable. Globalisation, migration, new knowledge and theories, as well as re-articulations of gender, race and sexuality among other social constructions, and developments in technology, are environmental forces for reshaping the social norms of touch. Social norms (can) shift, albeit often glacially-slowly, though sometimes rapidly at tipping points, of which digital touch technologies is one.

The contemporary moment of digital touch innovation means the social norms for their use are un-developed and in flux. This disrupts social touch norms, and offers a moment of social and cultural reflection, "fresh opportunities to think about our technologies, our connections and the relationships amongst them" (Baym 2015: 1). Technologies and people's use of them are mutually constitutive – they shape one another, accounting for the unexpected and emergent ways in which people take up and use the affordances and expectations of the technological, material and social: affordances that are built into the design of touch-based devices, systems, or environments. When these new technologies enter the 'Technoscape' (Appadurai 1990), societies reach a consensus over time and develop a set of norms and etiquette for their use. Central to this is how touch technologies engineer types of sociality whilst alongside this their users are developing norms around their use (van Dijck 2013). These shifting norms carry over into other domains to shape the ways people communicate and what is considered socially acceptable. With each new technology, the process begins again (Licoppe 2004). For example, the "gendering of humanoid robots, whether with intentional design cues or not, will likely perpetuate aspects of certain human-human roles and the ideologies that go with them" (Carpenter et al. 2009: 264). Consideration of the social norms of touch is therefore significant for the use and design of digital touch– whether attempting to work with, against or to reconfigure them.

4.3 Digital Touch and Social Norms

To illustrate the role of social norms in digital touch research and design, this section explores how touch norms are embedded in/actualized through the design and use of digitally mediated touch communication. To focus this discussion, we attend to digital touch for personal relationships, a primary domain for both the performance of gender (intimately tied to sexuality), culture, and the development of digital touch devices, systems and environments. We discuss this landscape through four interconnected aspects of touch implicated in the research and design of digital touch which are strongly governed by social norms: touching the body; types of touch; the materiality of touch; and touching practices.

4.3.1 Touching the Body

Social norms regulate where we touch ourselves and others. This is wrapped up into the concept of 'Body accessibility', that is, our willingness to let others touch our body (Jourard 1966). The most 'accessible' regions of the body to touch in Western cultures are the hands, head, and arms, the least accessible region are, unsurprisingly, the genitals. The context and closeness of a relationship correlates with where someone can be touched (Suvilehto et al. 2015). For example, women are more discriminating about where on their body they are touched, while men are more concerned with "the type of touch than the area of the body touched." (Moore et al. 2014: 44). Social norms of touch and body accessibility also pervade research studies on touch, with most studies performed on the hands (45%) and fingers (34%) (Gallace and Spence 2014: 335). Through a combination of social, physiological, technological reasons these body touch norms are echoed in the design of digital touch on the body, which primarily focus on the finger(s), hand, wrist, forearm, arm, with occasional forays to the torso and back (Huisman 2017).

The sense that the body is vulnerable through touch communication resonates across the InTouch case studies. Early student projects collected during the *Designing Digital Touch* case study, for instance, reflected the social norms of touch, with over a half locating touch on the hand or arm. While some engaged with other body parts, only a few engaged touch with the whole-body. The prototypes made during *Imagining Remote Personal Touch* case study, engaged with the body to different extents. While some prototypes echoed the norms of the touching finger or hand associated with the screen, established through commercial products and industry trends, others separated the body into specific socially 'low risk' 'accessible' touch communicative zones, some extended touch beyond the hand and forearm to the face (ear and cheek) and feet, and several brought the whole body into the non-sexual touch experiences that they provided. The 'Haptic Chair' prototype, for example, offered a whole-body sensorial touch experience in which a person was enveloped in an expanding material to create a sense of a hug: "*someone touching you is a 'soft' experience, more about heat than movement, with pressure, but not too much. The idea of 'someone being there', of being gently held 'contained'*" (Fig. 4.1).

Indeed, bringing in the wider body, even if moving beyond the hand, up the arm, across the shoulder, raised participants' concerns about the appropriateness and control of touch. The location of touch on the body, the body in general and issues of controlling touch, were of serious concern for participants. The group who made

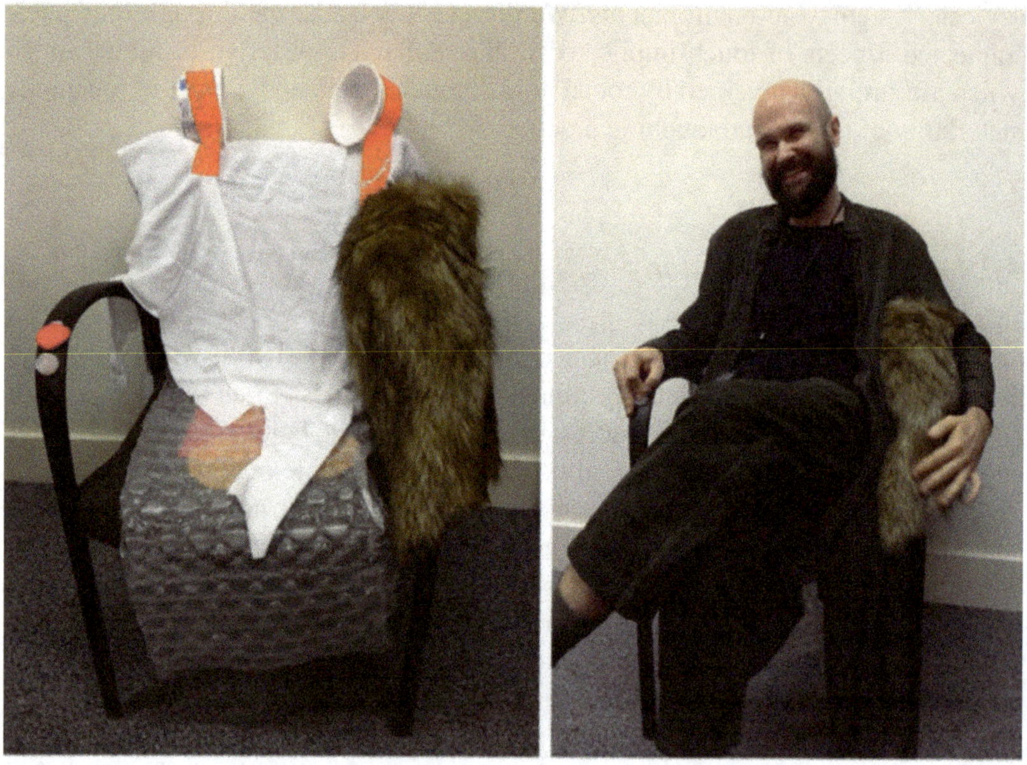

Fig. 4.1 The 'Haptic Chair' prototype offers a whole-body sensorial touch experience to create a sense of a remote digital hug, Imagining Remote Personal Touch case study

the 'Touch-cape' prototype, designed to send a 'hugging' digital touch to the upper-torso of the receiver wearing the cape, were concerned about the potential for a wearer to place the cape elsewhere, notably across their genitals. Such concerns led to much debate about the ambiguity and risks of digital touch, and led to the addition of layers of authenticating buttons and processes. The tension between public and private touch was repeatedly articulated through the body and a site for its regulation: much appeared to be at stake in the breaking of social norms of touch and imagining future digital touch brought this to the fore of participants' discussions and designs.

Locating touch on the body raises the question of what kinds of bodies are considered in the design and imagination of digital touch. The majority of the prototypes made in the *Imagining Remote Personal Touch* case study, were developed in relation to imagined gendered and sexual bodies, themes implicitly explored through discussion of age, gender and culture via discussions of size and the social acceptance or appropriateness of touch. This and other case studies inferred relatively 'fit', 'available' 'healthy' bodies, suggesting that some bodies are more readily thought of as 'for touching' in the context of personal relationships (as opposed to the context of health care). This normative body would appear to be the mental mannequin for the design of much touch technology.

4.3.2 Types of Touch

Digital touch for interpersonal relationships is imagined into lives and contexts that reflect gendered social norms of relationships including parenting, embedded in healthy, active successful lifestyles and personas. The potential of digital touch to increase connection, support communication, reduce stress and be time-efficient are foregrounded across the literature, prototypes, and our case studies. Digital touch is strongly co-opted into the risky work of managing personal relationships, particularly at long-distance. A variety of touch routines and repertoires populate the landscape of digital touch for personal relations, spanning from mobile hugging apps to sex robots. In a recent review of digital devices to support long distance relationships, for instance, 13 of 17 had some form of touch capacity. Beyond the sex toys littered across the digital landscape, the field of interpersonal digital touch is dominated by three everyday types of interpersonal touches: handshakes, kisses, and hugs. How have these three types of interpersonal touch have been digitalised?

The ubiquitous, seemingly banal gesture of the handshake in contemporary Western society is more than a physical-technical interaction, it is "simultaneously an embodied ritual, form of intimate touch, and legal gesture" an "important intersubjective and social gesture, communicating considerable amounts of information about and between the participants and their contexts, and both governed by and reproducing a variety of social norms" (Hamilton 2017: 55). This everyday touch of holding or shaking hands has been translated into several devices, including: 'Flex-N-Feel: Emotive Gloves' that support affective touch through vibrotactile sensations (Singhal et al. 2017); 'Frebble', a wireless accessory that lets you hold someone's hand from anywhere in the world (Toet et al. 2013); and 'Your Glove, Hot Hands and Hot Mits' (Gooch and Watts 2012), which realises handholding and hand-shaking behaviours through movement and heat. Interfaces can also simulate the feel of a virtual hand or object, its texture and elasticity, which encourages a sense of presence and supports collaboration (Kim et al. 2004). The immediate intimacy of holding hands or incidental touch, has been transformed into the squeeze of the Hey bracelet, sending the feel of your heartbeat via an Apple Watch, or the real-time feel of your partner's heartbeat via the HB ring. In our case study, *Art of Remote Contact*, the artists developed a digital art installation experience 'I wanna hold your hand', which visitors to the Remote Contact exhibition could interact with (see Chap. 1 for more information). The artefact was made in response to working with a couple, one of whom was living with dementia, and their love of walking and holding hands. The piece consisted of a pair of digitally-enabled gloves, embedded with Galvanic Skin and pressure sensors and GPS, and attempted to capture something of the experience of gradually noticing the shifting balance of their hand touching from romantic to supportive to care-giving as the partner's dementia progressed. Linked to an Arduino plotter that mapped the data collected in what one visitor called a 'map of affection' (Fig. 4.2).

Digital touch qualities and affordances can be altered and exploited in ways not possible in the 'real world'. A touch can be recorded, replayed, and manipulated, for

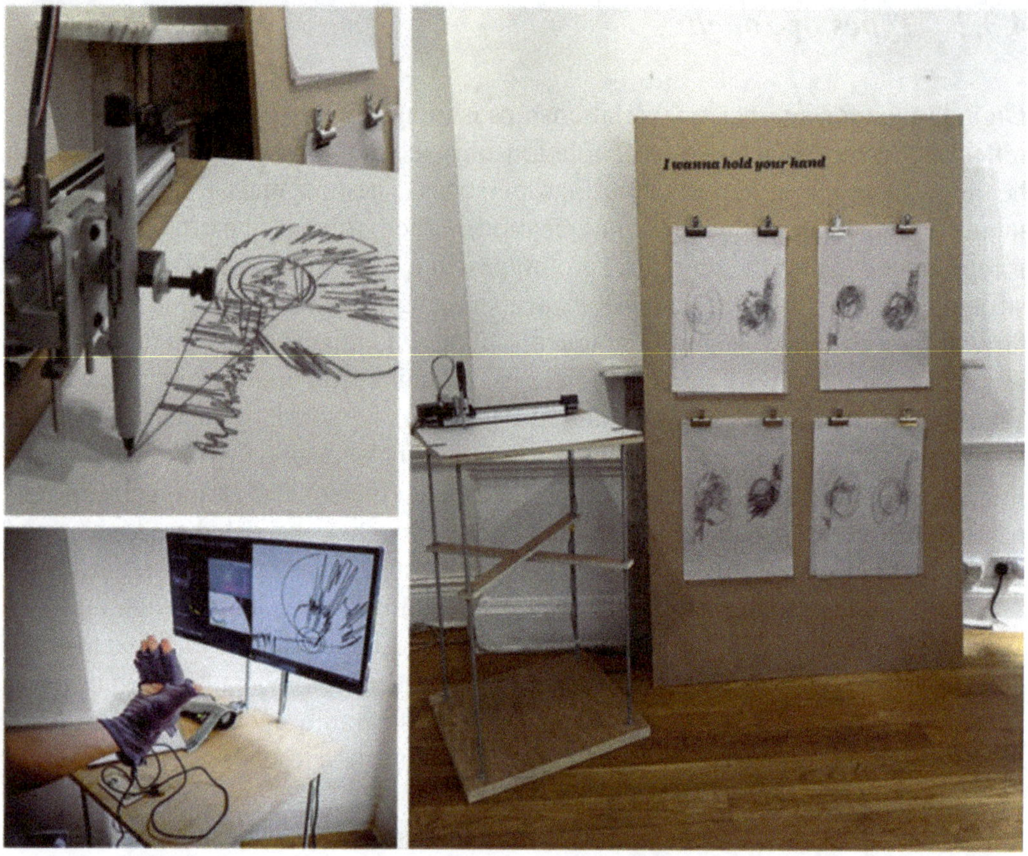

Fig. 4.2 The Remote Contact exhibition 'I wanna hold your hand' artefact, traced the experience of a joint walk, holding hands, via a pair of digitally-enabled gloves. Embedded galvanic skin and pressure sensors and GPS linked to an Arduino plotter that mapped the data collected. (Photo Credit Ed Waring)

example, one's handshake "can be made firmer if another person prefers a firmer handshake" (Bailenson et al. 2007: 348). These examples suggest that while touch, here a handshake, can move into the digital realm and even when severely degraded it can remain meaningful touch, there are significant losses (e.g. of social meaning, authenticity, and sensorial qualities) as well as gains (e.g. providing the possibility to shake hands with a remote other, manipulating touch, recording and replaying touch) in the remediation process. All of which raises new questions for what it actually means to shake hands. A digital handshake is a felt experience that can give a sense of connection but it is less easy to assess what, if any, information it communicates about and between people, and whether it fulfil the demands of the ritual. Similarly, it is difficult to know if the social norms (e.g. of gender) persist in this digital shake.

Kissing, "with its close body contact and erotic associations… is a prominent focus for both enactment and regulation" (Finnegan 2014: 207). We learn who, when, and where (both in terms of social context and the parts of the body involved – hand, cheek, nose, mouth and beyond) it is appropriate to kiss (Goffman 1963: 167). The norms of gender and power relations shape the meaning of a kiss, from love,

Fig. 4.3 The Kissenger, a prototype device for remote kissing, was used as a technological probe in the Imagining Remote Digital Touch case study

attachment, affection, deference, through to submission. As we age, and move beyond our familial cultural norms, and as cultural norms shift, what kissing is deemed appropriate changes. Like handshakes, kissing is a cultural practice, the number of cheek-kisses varies across cultures (one in Mexico, three in the Netherlands, two in France with some variation related to intensity of the friendship). In some cultures, kissing remains exclusively in the sphere of intimacy, and is not considered legitimate or decent in public. Romantic kissing is most common in the Middle-East and Asia and least common of all among Central American cultures, and around half of cultures have no evidence or knowledge of romantic kissing (Jankowiak et al. 2015).

Kisses can be sent and shared via Kissenger (Kiss Messenger), an interactive device that attaches to a mobile phone to provide a physical interface for transmitting a 'kiss' between two remotely connected people – the force that a user applies to a pair of lips is recreated on the other device using motors – and designed to augment video chat with the aim to promote intimacy in long distance relationships (Samani et al. 2012; Zhang and Cheok 2016). *CheekTouch* (Park et al. 2016) attaches to phones enabling people to send tactile signals – like kissing or stroking the cheek. But is it kissing? We used Kissenger as a technological probe in the *Imagining Remote Digital Touch* case study. Participants commented that '*it's a different experience, a different type of kissing*' and '*not the same as a real kiss*', but they agreed it is '*still like a kiss*'. The 'realness' of the digital kiss was made apparent when discussing whether it would be 'cheating' to digitally kiss another person with the device, which it was felt it would be. However, while digital kissing was not considered real it did mediate contact that was marked as considered to be socially taboo and deviant: two heterosexual men kissing. It seems likely that sustained digital mediation of activities that are considered outside of social norms will serve to remake those norms or rethink the social significance of an activity (Fig. 4.3).

A range of devices support hugging via apps, contracting rings and digitally augmented clothing (Schirmer et al. 2011; Rahman et al. 2010). These devices make a variety of qualities and affordances of touch available including pressure, duration, speed, temperature, vibration, and movement. How these are calibrated, configured and organised creates different touch patterns – hard, quick, long (intense touch); soft, slow, short (gentle). These draw social norms into view in the ways that they are taken up and interpreted by users, drawing on their relationship, context, gender and cultural norms of touch, alongside their personal histories. Touch can transmit emotion, even with touch "cues that are extremely degraded (Bailenson et al. 2007: 348)". The difficulty of moving beyond standard digital touch forms, swiping, tapping, vibration, and the use of touch as 'activating a feature' dominated the *Designing Digital Touch* case study. Even when digital touch was reduced to vibration, however, touch was talked of as gentle, weak, firm, too strong, holding, caressing, nice, unpleasant, a stroke, or a hug. It was attributed with social meanings – caring touch, comforting, playful, rejecting, loving, supportive touch, or controlling touch. Digital touch was seen as having the potential to fulfil social to intimate touch needs, with 'the right amount of touch' being key – understanding when pressure and duration moved from supportive to 'too much' through to 'aggressive or violent'. For some participants, interpretations of touch involved gendered associations and the creation of masculine and feminine touch, and attributing technology itself with a gender.

Participants in *Imagining Remote Digital Touch*, and *Tactile Emoticon* explored the idea of recording hugs and how that might feel. One group produced the idea of a tactile '*body message*' that records taps, movements, the '*shape of the body and its impression*', via pressure and heat, that could be re-played and felt. This shifted the temporality of touch from a simultaneous mutual exchange to an individual experience, opening the potential of a touch device without the necessity of a connection to others – positioning digital touch (or self-touch) on the cusp of an idealized mimicry of connection and an isolating experience. It raised ethical issues of using, storing and sharing recorded digital touch, particularly around consent and ownership of a touch, and brought the authenticity and safety of touch into question. As one participant said, "*If all hugs will feel the same – how will people distinguish?*" Participants agreed on the need to build in mechanisms for people to signal consent, rejection and withdraw from touch. The question of whether they should be able to change a touch that they received (e.g. make it stronger or weaker, or receive it on an unintended part of the body) was contentious, highlighting the ambiguity of digital touch, social norms of touch consent and the management of touch misunderstandings (also see Chap. 7).

4.3.3 The Materiality of Touch

The materiality of digital touch is a part of the technological affordances that both constrain and offer possibilities for what people can do (and mean). These are shaped by social and cultural histories and contexts of use in which the relationship between people and technology is cyclical and interconnected (Hutchby 2001). The relationship between materiality, the affordance of a technology and the interface a user is presented with and acts through is therefore a significant aspect of their communicational experiences. InTouch asks how this relationship plays out in the context of digital touch norms, and the relevance of materiality and affordances for the 'feel' of digital touch communication. On the one hand, materialities, including those of the body, are central to the take-up, subversion, disruption, and re-shaping of both touch and technological affordances. On the other, the ongoing process of digital dematerialization is seen to have disengaged with, and neglected the values of, the physical world (bodies, artefacts and interactions) to reduce or remove touch from the communicational environment (Van Campenhout et al. 2016).

Materiality is a resource used in the gendering of the digital touch landscape, it can be felt in the textual design of devices, and the provenance of materials – their historical uses that over time shape their gendered associations, meanings and values. A woman's touch, Classen argues (2005: 203), continues to evoke "women as media of softness, comfort and refinement, the symbolic and tactile counterpart to rough and tough men". Such forms of socially gendered touch are attached to and produced through material digital resources in the digital touch landscape: soft and smooth textures, vibrations, and sensations to materialise feminine touch (white or pastel in colour), and hard and rough used to materialise masculine touch (and dark in colour). The tactile qualities of materials are themselves gendered and changing. Devices that involve caring touch, are gendered through the contexts of their use, and their materiality – from soft robotics to the soft materiality, fleece fabrics and slowly inflating air pockets, of the T-Jacket designed to give a hug to "to calm, comfort and sooth the nerves of anyone who is stressed or anxious" (https://www.mytjacket.com/). In contrast, digital touch designed for contexts and markets of appeal to men, are actualised through hard plastic and vibration, as well as the user scenarios related to work and leisure. Emerging interfaces, such as *TanvasTouch* (Shultz et al. 2015), enable users to 'feel what you see' and imagine the development of 'textual emojis' through feeling texture of the digital online. For example, Gillet's 'Baby Face' digital and print campaign used *TanvasTouch* and the feel of sandpaper – a texture and resource associated with the 'masculine' practice of DIY, to convey the 'scratch' of a new father's beard on their baby (https://www.youtube.com/watch?v=RNfgK9b6sU8).

More generally, materiality is tied to the sentiment of 'it feels right'. The notion of 'feeling right' is entangled with the part of the body in contact with a device, the type of touch engaged with, and our non-digital experiences of gender and what it means to be human. Using Kissenger, for instance, requires users to hold the hard-plastic casing and press their lips, with some force, onto a soft plastic surface which sends a 'pattern of movement and pressure' to the other device/user. The multisensory nature of materiality was significant for *Imagining Remote Personal Touch* participants:

> It doesn't feel like a kiss, the texture is plastic, there is no warmth, and the rest of the device doesn't feel like a face, so it's like kissing a piece of plastic …it sounds very robotic.

Materiality is also key to the design of robotic touch, and touching robots: "A softer feel in and of itself may be pleasing or comforting to a person interacting with a robot, and may elicit a response of trust and openness" (Arnold and Scheutz 2017: 82). In other words, the material quality of a robot, the use of a hard-body or a soft-body, elicit different kinds of bodily presence and physical contact, so whilst sharing exactly the same programming, their performance may be fundamentally altered by their material differences. It is implied that soft interfaces may signal vulnerability (maybe also sensuality) in a way that hard robots do not, raising the question of interaction (see Chap. 3) and how soft robots may be gendered by users and the ethics of interaction (see Chap. 7).

Materiality is brought differently into question in Virtual Reality (VR) environments where typically inferred sensations of 'touch' are derived from visual graphics, or linked to controllers (e.g. gloves) and other haptics devices that can convey different kinds of haptic feedback. Furthermore, in VR environments the features and behaviours of objects related to the impact of touch (e.g. fragility, plasticity, decay, destruction, death, to name a few), are programmable in novel ways. These properties are designed differently across VR spaces, designers are reconfiguring the expressive potentials of touch, while users need to work to negotiate the volatility of its potential meanings in the virtual world. This opens up a space for generating different types of touch (if something fragile no longer breaks you can squeeze it, stretch it, throw it). As a result of this reconfiguration and virtual materiality, the types and norms of touch in the virtual world, can differ from those of the physical world. This poses challenges for users related to the negotiation of the social norms, rules, and types of touch that apply in the space of digitally mediated touch in VR where the boundaries between touch in the virtual and the physical world are blurred and in flux.

4.3.4 Digital Touching

As already discussed, norms evolve and become established over time. How does digital touch challenge or change critical aspects of touch-based communication and what kind of communication practices can emerge around it? There is a continual tension and negotiation between social norms at the level of society and culture, and individual practices at the level of lived lives. This tension can be productive, creating both moments of social stability and fluidity that influence social norms. The changing use of technologies and communicative resources – the resources, tools, processes and contexts that our uses of technologies open up, are central to the remaking of social norms (Jewitt et al. 2016). In this unstable and shifting landscape, social norms are disrupted, broken, changed and re-made through social interactions over time.

Social norms governing body accessibility persist in human-robot touch indicating the social and socialising power of touch "the extent to which people treat the act of touching body regions as a sign of closeness – even if the body belongs to a robot" (Li et al. 2017: 119). This emphasises the importance of designers accounting for socially appropriate design of touch (ibid). Using the Kissenger, as a technological probe provoked embarrassment and unease for participants. Their

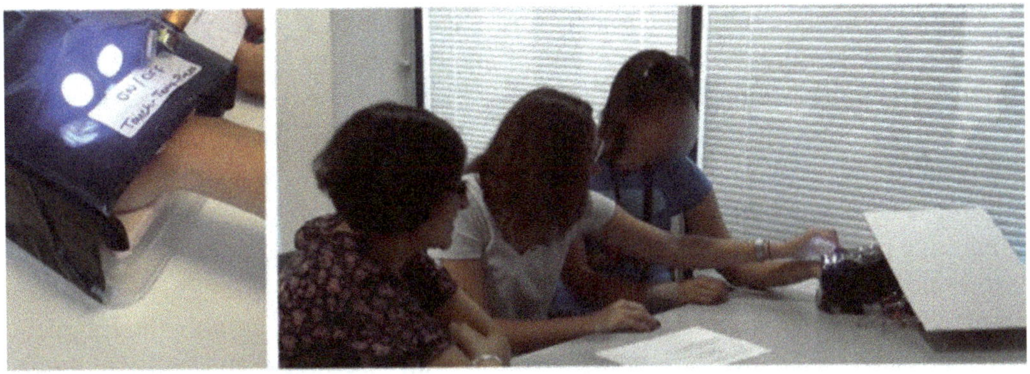

Fig. 4.4 The participants use the 'heat dial' of an early prototype Tactile Emoticon device to regulate the temperature of the tactile message

interaction marked kissing as a gendered (hetero-) normative practice – even when mediated by a machine. Devices such as Kissenger, also raise questions of whether, how and why future digital touch could continue or disrupt the work of gendering touch and what the consequences of failing to navigate these digital touch norms, or choosing to subvert or violate their expectations might be.

The *Tactile Emoticon* case study, provided insight into how new digital touch practices and norms might emerge. For example, the symbolic use of temperature to communicate progressive closeness. Participants used the 'heat dial' of the device to regulate the temperature of the tactile messages they were sending gradually from cold to hot:

M1: when you're trying to communicate you just want to be cold sort of
M2: Nothing too active. Just being together
M2: Let's make it like this let's start from a very very cold space at the beginning
M1: So, you want to give the sensation of getting warmer by the time
M2: Exactly yes
M1: Makes sense (she puts her hand into the device) …
M2: You can touch a bit and then make it a little bit warmer (they turn a button). Shall I turn it back (turns the button to cool) we don't love you that much anymore (they laugh) (Fig. 4.4)

Temperature is used to convey a gradual openness to touch: starting from a state of distance or non-touch ('very very cold') to a closeness, and the prospect of being touched. While warmth is a metaphor for closeness, the control and regulation of temperature afforded by digital touch is not a feature of physical touch.

The need to establishing communicative norms for what touch is wanted or unwanted appeared to be critical to participants across many of our case studies and was a focus of much concern echoing and referencing contemporary movements such as #MeToo, the social media campaign against sexual harassment. The digital touch features (i.e. heat, vibration, pressure) were used to generate and interpret a desire to connect or to be left alone. For example, in the *Tactile Emoticon* case study, the sending of a flat non-vibrating, no pressure and very hot touch was interpreted as an "off-putting tactile message" that is unpleasant to receive:

M2: Maybe they decided that they do not want to interact with us. Actually, they made it so hot to say – "Just leave me alone"

In the context of physical touch, unwanted touch is usually communicated through gaze, gesture, posture, movement and, sometimes, speech. In the absence of these communicative modes in the Tactile Emoticon the participants generated a new tactile communication practice: i.e. an off-putting message that made others not want to engage through touch. This practice can generate a set of norms involving, for example, conditions under which someone generates such a message. Is it something people do when they are angry or scared? What kind of rules might apply in this new practice that do not apply to physical touch? The underlying aspects involved in the generation of the 'Tactile Emoticon' message, notably the fragmentation of touch (regulating one element), the digitally mediated physicality of touch, and the use of what some participants called "unnatural functionalities" (i.e. turning a button to regulate temperature, vibration) reconfiguring the characteristics of touch communication.

4.4 Conclusion

Attending to the social norms that underpin people's touch interaction and communication, and how these are negotiated in social encounters provides a starting point from which to leverage understanding of the sociality of the tactile regime in which they are embedded. Social norms of touch developed in relation to 'direct' touch, and its associated etiquettes and practices, have been (and will be) brought into the use and design of digital touch devices, systems and environments, albeit in uneven ways. Like digitally mediated visual communication, some norms and practices will be disrupted in 'translation', and it is likely that some new touch capacities and interactions will be elicited. In this fluid mix, unintended and unexpected consequences for how we communicate with others via touch will emerge.

This highlights new opportunities for researching and designing digital touch communication that move beyond an emphasis on design explorations and point solutions towards a "deeper theoretical understanding of the presumed effects of mediated social touch on the social interaction process… to provide structure to the design space of social touch systems…guide the empirical experimentation process, as well as the interpretation of observed effects (or the lack thereof)" (Haans and Ijsselsteijn 2006: 155). Touch norms are significant in that they provide insights into the shared usage of touch for making culturally shared meaning of touch, and expectations of touch, which supports the imagination and design of digital touch communication.

Understanding and reflecting on our own touch norms, as well as those of the people we research or design for, is one route to recognising and benefiting from the potentials for difference and cultural flexibility towards new possibilities for designing digital touch communication. While on the one hand, understanding touch within the cultural complexities of the contemporary communicational landscape, characterised as it is by super-diversity, challenges the concept of social norms as stable and universal; on the other, gendered and cultural norms persist, perhaps more than ever given the hegemonic effect of the global circulation of technology. Social norms of touch are designed into and realised through the affordances of digital technologies. An awareness of the social norms of touch and how these regulate touch practices can help us to question, and/or engage newly with touch, from the mundane vibration of a phone in our pocket, to robotic-touch, and the innovation of contactless touch: the who, what, where, how and when of digital touch.

References

Appadurai A (1990) Disjuncture and difference in the global cultural economy. Publ Cult 2:1–24
Arnold T, Scheutz M (2017) The tactile ethics of soft robotics: designing wisely for human-robot interaction. Soft Robot 4(2):81–87
Bailenson JN, Yee N, Brave S, Merget D, Koslow D (2007) Virtual interpersonal touch: expressing and recognizing emotions through haptic devices. Hum Comput Interact 22:325–353
Baym N (2015) Personal connections in the digital age. Polity Press, Malden
Butler J (2004) Undoing gender. Routledge, London
Carpenter J, Davis JM, Erwin-Stewart N, Lee TR, Bransford JD, Vye N (2009) Gender representation and humanoid robots designed for domestic use. Int J Soc Robot 1:261–265
Chung LC (2019) Crossing boundaries: cross-cultural communication. In: Keith KD (ed) Cross-cultural psychology. Wiley, Chichester, pp 375–397
Classen C (ed) (2005) The book of touch, sensory formations Oxford. Berg, New York
Cranny-Francis A (2011) Semefulness: a social semiotics of touch. Soc Semiot 21:463–481
Field T (2003) Touch. MIT press, Massachusetts, MA
Finnegan RH (2014) Communicating: the multiple modes of human communication, 2nd edn. Routledge/Taylor & Francis Group, London/New York
Foucault M (2002) Archaeology of knowledge. Routledge, London
Gallace A, Spence C (2014) In touch with the future: the sense of touch from cognitive neuroscience to virtual reality. Oxford University Press, Oxford
Goffman E (1963) Stigma: notes on the management of spoiled identity. Simon & Schuster, London
Goffman E (1979) Gender advertisements. Palgrave, London
Gooch D, Watts L (2012) YourGloves, hothands and hotmits: devices to hold hands at a distance. In: Proceedings of the 25th annual ACM symposium on user interface software and technology – UIST '12. Presented at the 25th annual ACM symposium. ACM Press, Cambridge, MA, p 157
Haans A, Ijsselsteijn W (2006) Mediated social touch: a review of current research and future directions. Virtual Real 9(2–3):149–159
Halberstam J (2018) Trans∗: a quick and quirky account of gender variability. University of California Press, Oakland
Hall E (1966) The hidden dimension. Random House, New York
Hamilton SN (2017) Rituals of intimate legal touch: regulating the end-of-game handshake in pandemic culture. Sens Soc 12:53–68
Huisman G (2017) Social touch technology: a survey of haptic technology for social touch. IEEE Trans Haptics 10:391–408
Hutchby I (2001) Technologies, texts and affordances. Sociology 35:441–456
Jankowiak WR, Volsche SL, Garcia JR (2015) Is the romantic-sexual kiss a near human universal?: is the romantic-sexual kiss a near human universal? Am Anthropol 117:535–539
Jewitt C, Bezemer J, O'Halloran K (2016) Multimodal research. Routledge, London

Jonsson F, Lundmark S (2014) An interaction approach for norm-critical design analysis of Interface design. In: CaTaC'14, ninth international conference on culture, technology, communication, Oslo, Norway

Jourard S (1966) An exploratory study of body-accessibility. Br J Clin Psychol 5:221–131

Kim J, Kim H, Tay BK, Muniyandi M, Srinivasan MA, Jordan J, Mortensen J, Oliveira M, Slater M (2004) Transatlantic touch: a study of haptic collaboration over long distance. Presence Teleop Virt 13:328–337

Li JJ, Ju W, Reeves B (2017) Touching a mechanical body: tactile contact with body parts of a humanoid robot is physiologically arousing. J Hum Robot Interact 6:118

Licoppe C (2004) 'Connected' presence: the emergence of a new repertoire for managing social relationships in a changing communication technoscape. Environ Plann D Soc Space 22(1):135–156

Linden DJ (2016) Touch: the science of hand, heart, mind. Penguin, New York

Moore NJ, Hickson M, Stacks DW (2014) Nonverbal communication: studies and applications, 6th edn. Oxford University Press, New York

Park YW, Bae SH, Nam TJ (2016) Design for sharing emotional touches during phone calls. Arch Des Res 29(2):95–106

Rahman ASMdM, Hossain SKA, Saddik AE (2010) Bridging the gap between virtual and real world by bringing an interpersonal haptic communication system in second life. In: 2010 IEEE international symposium on multimedia. Presented at the 2010 IEEE international symposium on multimedia (ISM), IEEE, Taichung, Taiwan, pp 228–235

Remland MS, Jones TS, Brinkman H (1995) Interpersonal distance, body orientation, and touch: effects of culture, gender, and age. J Soc Psychol 135:281–297

Rode JA (2011) A theoretical agenda for feminist HCI. Interact Comput 23:393–400

Samani H, Parsani R, Rodriguez L, Saadatian E, Dissanayake K, Cheok A (2012) Kissenger: design of a kiss transmission device. DIS2012. Newcastle

Schirmer A, Teh KS, Wang S, Vijayakumar R, Ching A, Nithianantham D, Escoffier N, Cheok AD (2011) Squeeze me, but don't tease me: human and mechanical touch enhance visual attention and emotion discrimination. Soc Neurosci 6:219–230

Shultz C, Peshkin M, Colgate J (2015) Surface haptics via Electroadhesion: expanding Electrovibration with Johnsen and Rahbek. https://doi.org/10.1109/WHC.2015.7177691.

Singhal S, Neustaedter C, Antle AN, Matkin B (2017) Flex-N-feel: emotive gloves for physical touch over distance. In: Companion of the 2017 ACM conference on computer supported cooperative work and social computing – CSCW '17 companion. Presented at the companion of the 2017 ACM conference. ACM Press, Portland, pp 37–40

Suvilehto JT, Glerean E, Dunbar RIM, Hari R, Nummenmaa L (2015) Topography of social touching depends on emotional bonds between humans. Proc Natl Acad Sci 112:13811–13816

Toet A, van Erp JBF, Petrignani F, Dufrasnes MH, Sadhashivan A, van Alphen D, Boeree F, de Gruijter HO, Hoeksema J, Stamhuis CT, Steenbergen PJ (2013). Reach out and touch Somebody's virtual hand: affectively connected through mediated touch. In: 2013 Humaine Association conference on affective computing and intelligent interaction. Presented at the 2013 Humaine Association conference on affective computing and intelligent interaction, pp 786–791

Van Campenhout LDE, Frens J, Hummels C, Standaert A, Peremans H (2016) Touching the dematerialized. Pers Ubiquit Comput 20:147–164

Van Dijck J (2013) The culture of connectivity: a critical history of social media. Oxford University Press, Oxford

van Erp JBF, Toet A (2013). How to touch humans: guidelines for social agents and robots that can touch. In: 2013 Humaine Association conference on affective computing and intelligent interaction. Presented at the 2013 Humaine Association conference on affective computing and intelligent interaction, pp 780–785

West C, Zimmerman DH (1987) Doing gender. Gend Soc 1:125–151

Zhang EY, Cheok AD (2016) Forming intimate human-robot relationships through a kissing machine. In: Proceedings of the fourth international conference on human agent interaction – HAI '16. Biopolis. ACM Press, Singapore, pp 233–234

Links

Gillet Baby Face Advert. https://www.youtube.com/watch?v=RNfgK9b6sU8

T-Jacket. https://www.mytjacket.com/

Chapter 5
Touch Presence, Absence and Connection

Abstract Technologies are intrinsically linked to the ways in which physical, temporal and emotional distances are thought of and managed. Likewise, social relations and communication technologies mutually shape each other as they are developed and maintained. This chapter explores the social connections that digital touch technologies are beginning to shape, with a focus on the related experiences of presence and absence through mediated touch and the questions this raises for the design space of interpersonal relationships, that is, the mediation of touch between people. We first consider how these concepts have been defined and addressed in the literature on communication technologies in general, and touch technologies in particular. We then use three extended examples from InTouch case studies to explore and reflect on these concepts. We consider how touch technologies might challenge us to think about the interaction between human and machine. We close with a consideration of design implications and possibilities for future research.

Keywords Connection · Absence · Presence · Distance · Social relationships · Interpersonal · Isolation · Tactile emoticon · Bio-sensing · Parent-Infant Interaction

5.1 Introduction

Technologies are intrinsically linked to the ways in which physical, temporal and emotional distances are thought of and managed. Likewise, social relations and communication technologies mutually shape each other as they are developed and maintained. Baym (2015) refers to this as the 'social shaping' perspective (cf. Mackenzie and Wajcman 1999), a middle ground between technological determinism (technology influences society) and social constructivism (society influences technology). She argues that new or emerging media offer 'fresh opportunities' for social and cultural reflection, allowing us 'to think about our technologies, our connections, and the relationships amongst them' (Baym 2015: 1). And '[t]he very

C. Jewitt et al., *Interdisciplinary Insights for Digital Touch Communication*, Human–Computer Interaction Series,
https://doi.org/10.1007/978-3-030-24564-1_5

existence of interactive media that connect people across space gives rise to new connections' (ibid: 172).

Communication at a distance has advanced in speed, ubiquity and importance since the advent of modern communication technologies and in light of a global and increasingly (albeit unevenly distributed) mobile economy (Dimmick et al. 2011; Stafford 2004). The affordances, practices and evolving social relations emerging through and shaped by social networking sites (e.g. Facebook) and audio-visual communication platforms (e.g. WhatsApp, Snapchat, Skype or Facetime) have been brought into focus.

In this chapter, we explore the social 'connections' that digital touch technologies are beginning to shape, with a focus on the related experiences of presence and absence through mediated touch. We first consider how these concepts have been defined and addressed in the literature on communication technologies in general, and touch technologies in particular. We then use three extended examples from InTouch case studies to explore and reflect on these concepts. The InTouch project and case studies are introduced and outlined in Chap. 1. They include people's interactions and responses to a series of artistic technological provocations designed to enhance feelings of connection and tackle isolation in the Remote Contact exhibition; the social aspects of sending and receiving digital touch as a form of tactile support, drawing on our study of people's use of a prototype tactile emoticon; and parents' use of the Owlet Smart Monitor (OSS), a bio-sensing baby monitor and app, which we conceptualise as a form of mediated touch in the context of parent-infant interaction.

This chapter brings into focus the questions that touch technologies raise for the design space of interpersonal relationships, that is, the mediation of touch between people. We also consider how touch technologies might challenge us to think about the interaction between human and machine. We close with a consideration of design implications and possibilities for future research.

5.2 Connecting at a 'Distance': Questions of Presence

Within HCI, research on 'social presence' (also 'mediated social presence' or 'social telepresence' (Biocca et al. 2003: 459) has largely focused on the relative success of individual technologies to mediate human interaction, and on finding appropriate psychological or behavioural measures to assess this. Specifically, social presence theory has dealt with ways in which 'the "sense of being with another" is shaped and affected by [individual] interfaces' (ibid: 456), the perceived 'social richness' a medium might provide, or the extent to which it can generate key social measures, such as involvement, immediacy or intimacy (ibid: 465). According to Dimmick et al. (2011), social presence in mediated communication first received attention from researchers in the context of teleconferencing (Short et al. 1976), with a view to assessing 'how technology provides filters that add or subtract [verbal or nonverbal] cues found in unmediated social interaction' (Biocca et al. 2003:

472). It was the telecommunication context itself that problematised the notion of presence and absence as binary oppositions, making room for a 'continuum in which mediated others could be more or less present' (ibid: 460). This was also in parts influenced by Goffman's notion of 'co-presence' which, in social-interactionist terms, not only referred to physical presence but to the impact that presence (and 'the reception of embodied messages' (Goffman 1959: 15) had on individual actors' behaviours, and their assessment of the intentional states of others. Accordingly, co-presence did not simply refer to the 'sense of being with another' but its social and interactional implications (e.g. responses to social cues).

As Biocca et al. (2003: 456) explain, within HCI social presence theory, 'the other' can refer to 'either a human or artificial intelligence', as long as there is that sense of '*intelligence* suggesting broadly the notion of intentionality and intelligent behavior relative to the environment and the self' (ibid: 463, original emphasis); 'just the copresence of a body may not be a good definitional basis for social presence, but rather we could say that the body is a set of cues for an "intelligence" that animates it'.

Human communication is core to media and cultural studies scholars who broaden perspectives of mediated social presence to the social connections or relations that shape and are shaped by media technologies. Here, the notion of 'connecting' with others across distance (in its multiple connotations) opens up wider considerations of mediated, synchronous or imagined presence. That is, the ability to 'connect' with someone or something is understood to work on an emotional-intellectual level and does not need to be physical or even reciprocal. In the context of long-distance relationships, connection has often been discussed as a sense of 'togetherness' and the means by which to achieve this; people connect, technically, via a range of communication technologies to generate a feeling of human connectedness, of being 'together and to build on a form of togetherness via shared imagined future moments' (Cantó-Milà et al. 2016: 2409). Here, too, different communication technologies afford different ways of connecting. For instance, Licoppe (2004: 135f) evidences a gradual shift in which 'instead of being used [...] to compensate for the absence of our close ones, [they] are exploited to provide a continuous pattern of mediated interactions that combine into "connected relationships", in which the boundaries between absence and presence eventually get blurred'. An example is the change from longer domestic landline conversations to shorter, more regular interactions via mobile phones. He sees in this the emergence of a 'connected presence', in that the ongoing 'flow of irregular interaction helps to maintain the feeling of permanent connection, an impression that the link can be activated at any time' (ibid: 141). Similarly, Baym discusses O'Hara et al.'s (2014) description of 'everyday dwelling' where '[p]artners left video chat open ritualistically to hang out, eat together, watch TV together, or watch each other fall asleep' (Baym 2015: 158). She notes how 'kissing and sex, not surprisingly, worked best in person, although mock-kissing had its charms' (ibid), highlighting the physical restrictions of audio-visual communication technologies that have given force to imaginations of mediated touch, as outlined in more detail below. The nature and quality of connection in its technical sense still matters for communication, with bad or interrupted connections (e.g. latency issues or distortions) potentially leading to miscommunication or communication break-downs.

Beyond the notion of connected presence and 'co-presence by proxy' (e.g. visual content retrieved through social media), Madianou (2016) argues that it is multifaceted and dynamically negotiated 'polymedia' environments (cf. Madianou and Miller 2013) that facilitate a 'new, hybrid type of indirect co-presence', that is, 'ambient co-presence' (Madianou 2016: 187). She defines this as the 'increased awareness of the everyday lives and activities of significant others through the background presence of ubiquitous media environments' (ibid: 183); which relates also to 'ambient intimacy', coined by Hjorth et al. (2012) and discussed in Lambert (2016). Here, connection and presence (or absence) go beyond the nature and significance of individual communication interfaces or moments of mediated interaction to refer to the phenomenological experience of 'feeling' in touch (in this case, without actually touching) and to an imagined presence. This is akin to a more abstract notion of connecting that goes beyond establishing and maintaining contact to refer to people's ability to imbue connections with personal meaning at moments of co-located or remote interaction or imagining. In terms of this 'emotional' connection or connectedness, we might not only connect with people near and far but also with objects, ideas, or times, by becoming aware of and attributing meaning to them.

5.3 Connecting Through Touch

Touch has a special role in relation to human connectedness, and increasingly so as mediated social-sensorial experience. It has been seen as the 'point of connection' itself that helps us to 'know both the self and the other', and to differentiate between the two: '[i]n differentiating the other from ourselves, we are able also to connect knowingly with that other' (Cranny-Francis 2011: 468). From this perspective, connection is 'engagement', or a form of 'being with', that can be physical (through contact), emotional (feeling, empathizing), or intellectual (in terms of understanding or knowing) (ibid: 470). The three might overlap, as in the sense of excitement of touching an object from the past, that is, something that is personally, socially or culturally meaningful and 'links or connects us to that past' (ibid: 469). Museum-based research suggests that touch can establish essential connections of social, cognitive and therapeutic value (Chatterjee and Noble 2013), help visitors to build narrative connections with objects via their own experiences and memories (Jewitt and Price 2019), with visitors reflecting how touching artefacts provides a 'strong sense of their body meeting that of another person over an immense time and space' (Candlin 2010: 65).

Paterson (2006) extends this to interacting with virtual objects, exploring how (physical) distances both collapse and become differently meaningful through feelings of 'presence', 'co-presence' and 'immersion' (Paterson 2006: 691). To him, the immersion that is achieved through the collocation of haptic and visual feedback when touching virtual objects via haptic devices (e.g. the PHANToM) – of making the intangible (digital, virtual) quite literally tangible – gives a sense of realness and presence that vision alone cannot achieve (ibid: 698). It 'brings the distant into an almost phenomenologically felt near-space of proximity, while also maintaining that distance' (ibid: 703), allowing users to feel the "active presence of absent things"' (a quote attributed to Paul Valéry, see Thrift 2000: 222, in Paterson 2006: 697). A sense of distance remains because we know or imagine there to be physical distance, as in the case of the first 'virtual handshake' (actually an attempt at collaboratively manipulating a virtual object from both sides of the Atlantic),(Kim et al. 2004). But this 'distance is brought to life' (to paraphrase Josipovici, Paterson 2006: 696) through the tactile interaction with the haptic device. In the case of the virtual handshake, this was proof of achieving a sense of 'co-presence' (Kim et al. 2004) which, if extended to other relationships, may foster 'feelings of nearness and intimacy' (Paterson 2006: 693). In this context, the greater the fidelity of the haptic feedback/sensation, the greater is the sense of presence or co-presence.

To Paterson, writing at a time when haptic technologies were even more emergent, the feeling of touching the virtual object is so real, in fact, that he evokes Walter Benjamin's (1936) notion of 'aura', hitherto a quality integral to, or reserved for, original artefacts (rather than their copies/reproductions). 'The distances involved', Paterson writes, 'do not qualitatively affect the feeling of the manipulation process, the sense of presence of an object or copresence of another person' (Paterson 2006: 702). In other words, it is as though we felt the object (the original) itself, rather than its representation. Arguably, this is more complex an argument than Paterson suggests – not least because virtual entities do not necessarily need to be copies or representations of an 'original'. It is also questionable if the sensorial experience of the haptic device at hand (its own feel) can be completely ignored, no matter how high the fidelity of haptic sensation or how convincing the illusion of virtual touch. What is invoked, however, is the feeling of connection as immediate and intimate, suggesting an ability to actually grasp a thing at hand, or to 'feel' and make more 'real' and tangible the presence of a (distant) other.

Presence and immersion are key concepts in Immsersive Virtual Reality (VR). Specifically, immersion refers to the experience of spatial presence in the digital environment where the media contents are perceived and treated as real (Madigan 2010). Touch is seen as a critical element in achieving a high degree of presence in VR environments: 'Haptics is at the core in the way we interact with the our surroundings, and without it we will be never fully embodied in a virtual world' (Abrash 2015 in Parisi 2018: 188 loc.). In VR presence involves a sense of being there (in the virtual) and being able to act and interact in the virtual world in a way that is not only non-disrruptive but it is also experienced as real. In Social VR – where users are virtually embodied in the same virtual world – presence can take different forms in a spectrum from co-existence to connection. Connecting through engagement is a common activity in the virtual space (e.g. watching films together, playing games collaboratively and co-constructing virtual objects). However, the potential for connection in social VR can be violated (e.g. Harrassement) which raises the need to define and regulate unwanted touch.

Presence in VR refers mainly to the virtual space and emphasizes the bypassing of the physical space however, it also presupposes a physical body which experiences (multimodally and sensorially) the impact of actions and its presence in the virtual world. A critical element of VR presence is therefore the creation of a connection – at a conceptual and emotional level – between this physical body and the virtual world. Kozel (1994:3) notes of this connection: 'The famous claim associated with virtual technology is that the body is futile, replaced by an infinitely enhanced electronic construct. If this is so, then why did nastiness or violence enacted upon my image hurt? How could the body be futile yet still exert a basic visceral control over my movement?'. Digital mediation of touch in VR adds a physical dimension (e.g. feeling the touch between two avatars or the explosion of a bomb) to the sense of connection. The physicality of the mediated tactile experience is envisaged to produce a high-level (near complete) absorption of the physical body into the virtual world and in doing so, virtual touch has the potential to expand the range and the novelty of felt experiences.

As (Puig de la Bellacasa 2009: 305) argues, '[t]ouch technologies and dreams of being in touch match well', feeding into a market that reaffirms connecting and longing at a distance. At the time of writing this chapter, the majority of long distance relationship gadgets on the market involve some form of remote touch, from the transmission of lovers' heart beats (e.g. Apple Watch, Pillow Talk), via haptic devices for tactile messaging or gesturing (e.g. hugs, kisses, holding hands), to the use of connected sex toys (e.g. Lovense, Kiirroo, Vibease, see LastingTheDistance.com 2019). While some remain at the proof-of-concept or crowdfunding stages, others are becoming commercially available (e.g. HEY, Kissenger). The makers of Pillow Talk argue that being 'able to *feel* connected to our loved ones' is needed where 'emoticons and pixelated video calls just don't really cut it' (http://www.littleriot.com/pillow-talk/).

Recent research in affective digital touch, elsewhere refered to as 'affective haptics' (Eid and Osman 2016) or 'mediated social touch' (Huisman 2017; van Erp and Toet 2015) has highlighted the complexity of unpacking and digitizing touch for remote communication, demonstrating ambiguities in research results and limitations of existing solutions. Much focus has been on the effectiveness of transmitting specific types of touch and emotions (e.g. Obrist et al. 2015) or its role in multisensory/−modal communication (e.g. Park et al. 2016). Across these approaches, there is always – implicitly or explicitly – the underlying design challenge of touch as an embodied physical experience, addressing (parts of) the body as the locus of touch or integrating body location (e.g. different parts of the arm) in the touch recognition pattern.

In this context, 'social presence' has been aligned with interfaces' ability to create and convey touch convincingly and meaningfully, be this in the aforementioned context of interpersonal relations, gaming, collaborative working, or human-machine and human-robot interaction. With regard to the latter, van Erp and Toet (2015) cite a study on toddlers' interaction with a humanoid robot (Tanaka et al. 2007) which found that 'social connectedness correlated with the amount of touch between the child and robot' (van Erp and Toet 2015: 6), while another study noted that the 'warmth of a robotic hand mediating social touch contributed significantly to the feeling of social presence' (ibid 2015: 6), indicating the importance of 'human' touch qualities. Our InTouch case study on the Tactile Emoticon approached the area of affective or supportive touch exploratively in terms of the social aspects and relations at play in mediated touch communication. Here, focus was both on optimizing a touch interface and the ways in which participants imagined and made sense of remote personal touch through the device. As such, it was akin to a socio-technological probe study.

5.3.1 *Tactile Emoticon*

The *Tactile Emoticon* case study involved the development and qualitative exploration of a communication prototype for the transmission of touch through the synthesis of three tactile subcomponents – temperature, pressure and vibration – across two remotely connected devices. The devices were designed t send, receive or amalgamate touch messages. Six groups of two to three participants were invited to explore the device for purposes of supportive touch in relation to three scenarios: romantic love, pain and social rejection. While questions of connection, presence or absence were not always explicitly verbalised (as concepts), these were observed to be in play – at times, playfully so – across participants' tactile interactions and related discussion.

Participants' attempts to enable touch communication *as* connection – i.e. successfully transmitting and conveying a tactile message – was key to many interactions, with the physical distance between dyads of teams and the lack of other sensory cues creating challenges for interpretation and, conversely, a sense of disconnection: '*let's try to decode what they are saying… It is difficult to use this on its own, I could use it while speaking on the phone… I could support it with my body language, or words.*' Participants actively 'connected' and 'disconnected' through the device by the very placement and removal of their hands; to some, the presence and absence of communication partners became the clearest tactile 'message' transmitted through the device.

However, 'connection as presence' was not straightforwardly 'presence as connectedness'. Participants tested the device's affordances through 'disruptive practices', for instance by using extreme cold to communicate not wanting to be touched or to interrupt a specifically unwelcome tactile message (e.g. vibration or too much heat in acute pain or social rejection). While there is an element of looking for extremes to understand the device's functional limits and boundaries, participants' communicative choices (e.g. cold) indicated an attempt to transfer known sensory-social meanings into the digital touch context, thus maintaining and differently shaping communicative norms and social relations. This sometimes meant that embodied associations of touch moved from the activating/receiving hand to imagined whole-body interactions. For instance, pressure came to denote containment (as in a hug), and raised temperature was used to convey the warmth of holding somebody.

Part of emerging digital touch practices here was also the use of provocations (e.g. 'too hot' messages) to infer presence from the reaction of the others, in that no reaction signalled absence: '*I don't think they are there. Or if they are there, they are not moving their hands.*' Significantly, absence was not simply the lack of touch associated with the presence or absence of specific subcomponents (e.g. lack of vibration). It was also associated with seemingly undifferentiated (repeated or unchanging) messages, as though there was an element of 'absent-mindedness' akin to the mechanical reproduction of communication patterns.

Across the case studies, questions of presence and absence became key to interpreting both the workings of digital devices and instances of tactile communication. Importantly, the devices themselves became 'present' through their affordances and materiality. This is partly due to their relative novelty as a medium for communication, with participants having to work out rules and opportunities for the creation of patterns or recognizable signs. It is also linked to the sensorial interface itself that, for some, seemed too rubbery, 'synthetic' and 'artificial'. While a design aim might be to more directly, intuitively and conclusively mediate tactile messages, participant reflections on how best to communicate intent also highlighted questions of presence and absence as less on a continuum and more associated with specific acts of imagining the other, for instance in terms of 'by proxy' whole-body interactions (a touch of the hand evoking a hug) or touch partners' 'absent-mindedness' as indicated by the repetitiveness of touch patterns.

Besides the technical challenges of replicating human touch for affective support, the case study led us to reflect on the qualities and boundaries of touch in new ways. How do we signal unwanted touch in the absence of other cues? What does it take to authenticate the touch of a loved one? How do we know it is real? How easy would it be to replicate it, and to what consequence? The repetitive touch pattern itself may not only have suggested absent-mindedness but the absence of a body on the other end, with the machine continuing to entertain the mere illusion of presence (cf. Lombard and Selverian 2008: 319, who address adding physicality to the avatar of a deceased). Indeed, if it is part of a touch interface to make touch particularly 'real' or 'convincing', what stops it from becoming manipulative or fostering unwanted connections? Biocca et al. (2003: 469) mention the political implications of producing distance communication technologies that are *too* successful at social communication, in the sense that they might influence/persuade in the context of commerce or government propaganda. Similarly, Cranny-Francis warns that '[t]he connection generated when the human touches the machine might constitute the human as member of a technological assemblage, from which he/she derives power' (Cranny-Francis 2011: 469f) but 'where it occurs without full knowledge of the individual subject it may be harmful and disabling.' (ibid: 470). This is the case if tech users become 'incorporated into a technological entity or assemblage of which they may have limited knowledge and understanding' (ibid). This raises questions over how immersive, real or authentic we want touch technologies to be – or conversely, how transparent in their workings. We return to some of these issues in Chaps. 6 and 7, in relation to the sociotechnical imaginaries and ethics of digital touch.

5.4 Beyond the Interface

The intricacies of familiar interpersonal touch as they are known by those close to us came into focus in the *The Art of Remote Contact* case study. The touch provocations in the Remote Contact exhibition were designed to encourage particular forms of touch in co-located spaces, stretching notions of touch and rendering touch itself *present* – by making it visible, audible, graspable, and preservable. Significantly, visitor interaction and imagining engaged with presence, abence and connection beyond the affordances of the interface or specific moments of mediated touch interaction.

5.4.1 Remote Contact

The premise for the *Art of Remote Contact* case study and exhibition emerged out of the longing to connect in a context of perceived dis-connection – or reconfigured connections – brought about by the challenges of dementia. Invisible Flocks' creation of touch-based artefacts or provocations built on conversations and encounters with people living with dementia and their carers, in which touch had surfaced as central to communicating and being with each other (described in Chap. 1).

The exhibition partly encouraged the coming together of bodies, through physical contact or joint touch movements, and a range of ways of connecting through touch, sometimes quite literally so, encouraging touch between strangers or people who knew each other but were not used to holding hands, enabling people to be together differently. Visitors reflected on the experience of interacting with the *I wanna hold your hand* gloves and 'rain' exhibits, for example, describing the act of holding hands as 'quite romantic', or alternatively 'quite bizarre', noting that as friends they 'never hold hands', laughing uncomfortably at holding hands with a work-friend or stranger, or explicitly reflecting on the discomfort of holding hands or withdrawing from the act out of embarrassment at having sweaty-hands, as well as the power of doing so (Fig. 5.1):

> I work in care homes and people hold your hands a lot and can hold it for quite a long time, and you sometimes feel quite uncomfortable because you worry that you shouldn't be holding hands because they are not somebody who you know that well…A lot of people I work with you don't really have conversations, so handholding can be a real point of communication, you don't necessarily speak.

These reflections often led to discussions of imagining new forms of digital touch and how these might ameliorate or reconfigure them. And further, it played with the notion of the mutual shaping of technological, social and sensory touch connections.

Beyond touch connection as physical and technological 'contact', three themes emerged as central to our discussion here.

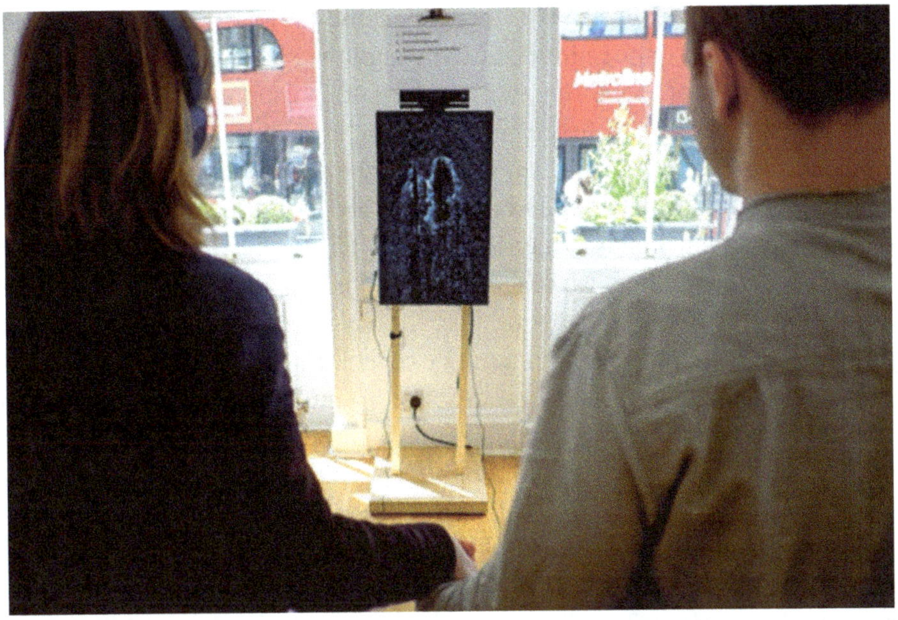

Fig. 5.1 The *I wanna hold your hand* gloves and 'rain' artefacts prompted visitors to the Remote Contact exhibition to hold hands, often with strangers. (Photo credit: Ed Waring)

Fig. 5.2 Visitors using the *Motion Prints* artefact engaged in playful touch with therapy putty, themselves and one another as a way of being together and connecting through touch and shared memories of tactile experiences. (Photo credit: Ed Waring)

First, the exhibition opened up questions of presence, absence and connection through emphasizing the temporal and emotional kinds of distance that can also be negotiated through touch. It resonated with visitors who had come to the gallery with personal and professional connections to people living with dementia. Visitors commented on being able to imagine using the *Motion Prints* artefact in (care) homes as a playful, tactile and intuitive way of being together and re-connecting where someone (or someone's previous identity) had felt absent. This was largely because it overcame perceived linguistic barriers. At the same time, visitors made relevant how the activity of working with the therapy putty evoked, and thus made present, memories of related, perhaps past creative practices, such as kneading dough or crafting (Fig. 5.2).

Second, in relation to the above, touch became part of connecting beyond the mediation of human-to-human touch and through the sharing of touch experiences, movements and memories. A sense of wanting to preserve and revisit the shared 'memory' and experience of touch moments lay the foundation for *I wanna hold your hand*. Within the context of the exhibition, the sensor-equipped gloves became an artefact for visitors to interact and document touch with; as they wore the glove, moved and flexed their hands, touched themselves or others, sensor data was displayed on screen and, at the push of a button, printed on a piece of paper which visitors could display in the gallery or take home. This made touch present and 'graspable' as a tactile (and visual) memory object. Similarly, touch became differently present through its translation (transduction) into other modes, such as sounds and light (*Water Synthesizer*) or sounds, visuals and joint movement (*Rain*).

Third, Remote Contact brought to the fore the role of the whole body – or different bodies – in seeking out or resisting social, sensory and emotional connections. For some, touch got in the way of social connections by foregrounding the presence of one's awkward body. This highlighted the need for touch technologies to be responsive to the diversity of bodily feeling and related social sensitivities of touch. Others found in *I wanna hold your hand* new ways of connecting with one's own body, through encouraging movement and self-touching, and again through making visible and present (through plotting and printing) what would otherwise remain invisible, albeit felt in differently embodied ways.

5.5 Touch Connection as a Bodily Way of Knowing

Touch as multifaceted mode of communication and bodily way of knowing through connecting were key themes emerging from our engagement with the Owlet Smart Sock (OSS) as an instance of digitally mediated touch. Questions over caregivers' presence and absence – and the managing of proximity and distance – are inscribed into discourses around baby monitors more widely. Here, they are partly amplified in the smart socks's potential to directly disrupt with a range of tactile interactions and connections with one's child. In this context, we approach the smart sock's skin contact and wireless transmission of physiological data to parents' smart devices as a form of remote touch, akin to some of the wider embodied practices caregivers use to check their baby's well-being: the hand on the chest to sense breathing, or moving across baby's body to assess their temperature, feeling baby's muscle tone through holding, and manipulating limbs to test baby's movements and sensations (Leder Mackley et al. under review). The *In Touch with Baby* case study contributes to an emerging body of research that seeks to get to the ontological experiences of parents and babies in understanding bodies and maintaining social relations through touch (Lupton 2013), with a focus on how these may be shaped at the introduction of a touch technology.

5.5.1 In Touch with Baby

On one level, 'connection', in the context of the OSS, meant something very practical or technical: positioning the (sufficiently charged) smart sock correctly on baby's foot to establish readings; remembering to turn on the base station to enable alerts; connecting smart sock and base station to transfer data via Bluetooth; sending data from base station to smart phone app via Wifi. These largely 'invisible' connections are vital to the successful functioning of the device. They can also be understood in relation to people's perceived sense of digital-material connections and flows as these are encountered and imagined as part of the home (cf. invisible architectures of which digital flows are a part, Pink et al. 2016). Walls and bodies could interrupt these flows, leading to a lack of technical and social connection.

On an interpersonal level, technical connections mattered, not least when they were difficult to achieve or interfered with existing parenting routines and touch interactions. In one case, handling the device itself led to stressful touch interactions with the baby, which jeopardised the overall goals of soothing the baby ready for bed. That is, while parents were present and interacting with their baby, their simultaneous interaction with the technology disrupted a sense of connecting or bonding through touch. The baby also seemed bothered by the material presence of the sock on their foot, seeking to kick it off. For this family, 'dis-connections' and resultant alerts led to interrupted sleep (Fig. 5.3).

Conversely, we observed parents establishing new interpersonal and experiential connections to their babies through a form of co-located remote touch. In unpacking parents' experience with the OSS, we found touch an important communicator of parental presence (and, with it, reassurance, love and protection – *'he likes to know you're there'*). It was also a significant part of soothing parents' own, at times anxious bodies. Touching one's child was a way of making their (healthy, breathing)

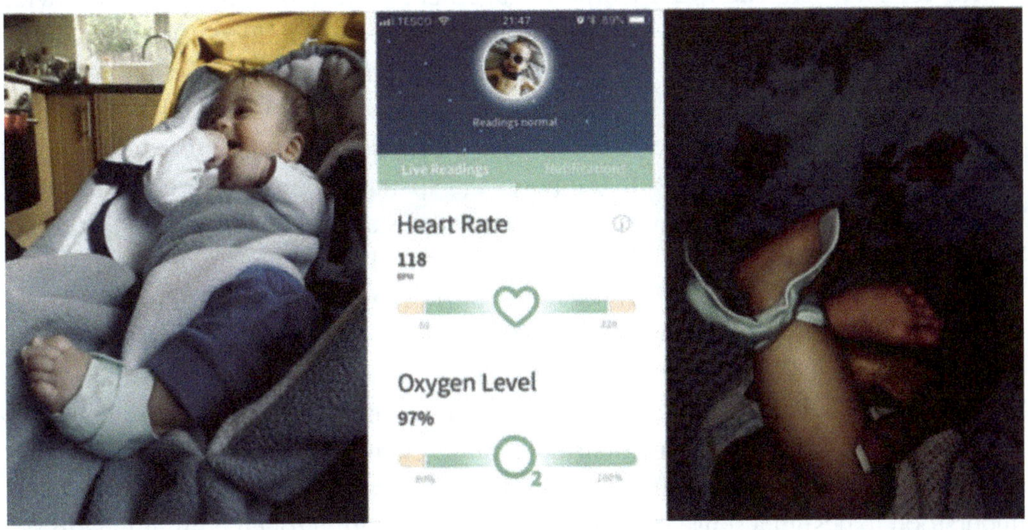

Fig. 5.3 Connecting parent and baby by positioning the Owlet Smart Sock correctly on baby's foot to establish readings on the app|On the right: an example of night time disconnections

bodies present. For one participant, Becky, who had lived with postnatal anxiety, the OSS was transformative in taking on a co-parenting (co-touching) role in this context. Initially, it meant that Becky did fewer physical checks on her son, which provoked mixed feelings. Later in the study, touch practices were resumed but had changed in their timing and quality; based on sensor readings, Becky trusted her baby to be well before going to check on him, hence reducing some of her anxiety. Getting more sleep had an overall positive impact on her and her baby's well-being and, by extension, their relations with each other. Through her monitoring and interpretation of readings, achieved through a form of digital touch, Becky found her son to be a 'good' baby in his ability to get to sleep on his own accord, which Becky saw unfold in his dropping heart rate as displayed on the Owlet app.

This is comparable to the experience of another mother, Susan, who saw in the OSS an opportunity to monitor her son's heart rate for quasi-diagnostic purposes (cf. Wang et al. 2017). This was a particular concern for her family as an older sibling lived with severe epilepsy; extreme fluctuations in baby's heart rate potentially indicated the same underlying condition. Here, a new sense of presence and absence, that of symptoms and related medical conditions, became pertinent to sensing baby's body through touch technology. As with Becky's new insights into the workings of her son's body (and similarly to Remote Contact's sensor-equipped glove), this form of digitally mediated touch made present bodies and bodily workings in new ways. However, there were moments when Susan's engagement with readings and the virtual representation of her baby led to a feeling of dis-connection with the baby that was, physically, present next to her. As these illustrative examples suggest, the OSS case study demonstrates the complexities of 'remote touch communication' in (near) co-located interaction, as at once interfering with social-experiential connections, and at once creating new ones.

In the case of the OSS, the significance and complex distribution of proximity and distance related to and influenced notions of presence, what is made present and absent for the user. The quasi-tactile engagement with babies through the Owlet sock and app made present what would otherwise remain hidden. Or rather, what would otherwise require near-proximity and a combination of visual, auditory and tactile checks (e.g. attending to blue lips, sunken chests, rapid breathing or heart beat) was now available more immediately, perhaps preventatively, on the app at some distance, reconfiguring both temporal and spatial dimensions. As was the case with Susan and Becky, of course, proximity and distance were relative; they could be near and feel distant, or (relatively) remote and feel close. The Owlet raises questions which are also pertinent to other forms of 'telecare' (e.g. remote surgical interventions). Here, Puig de la Bellacasa (2009) asks what happens when the rules of co-relationality and touch reversibility change and patients cannot attain who touches them, and she argues that new forms of connection can both produce co-presence and absence, and can redistribute, rather than reduce, distance. The experiences created by the balance and inter-relation of these different factors needs to be understood to design a sense of connection through digital touch communication.

5.6 Conclusion

In this chapter, we have discussed concepts of presence, absence and connection as these have been addressed in the communications and touch technology literature, and we explored how they manifested themselves across three InTouch case studies. Illustrations from the case studies demonstrate how 'connections' can be significant technologically, socially, communicatively, sensorially, emotionally and imaginatively. The case studies also show how people, technologies, bodies and memories can be differently present and absent in and through our interactions with digital touch technologies, and that such concepts as presence, absence and connection can change in valence. For instance, 'the potential to elicit feelings of social presence' because of its associations with 'physical interaction and co-location' (van Erp and Toet 2015: 2) is not straightforwardly a connecting presence, in the positive sense of human connectedness. While this significantly opens up the design space and scope of what we might mean by producing 'presence' and 'connection' through digital touch, this also suggests the need to attend to the situated social and sensorial meanings that emerge through interaction moments of which digital touch is a part.

Similarly, we see a number of tensions running through the literature and case studies which, rather than easily resolved, might serve as important considerations for design. First, there is a tension between the creation of presence/absence and connection through the successful transmission of tactile messages or the 'replication' of human touch on the one hand, and the idea that these concepts can also function on a symbolic and imagined level, or indeed may give rise to new forms of sharing, experiencing or knowing through touch. A related tension is one between the significance of individual touch interfaces – their materiality, sensorial affordances, social connotations and functionality – and the idea that these might move into the background and function as 'mere' mediators or enablers of digital touch communication.

Interfaces can be transformative or reductionist, depending on how advanced or situationally appropriate they 'feel'. And they are strengthened by being sensitive to differently situated and experiencing bodies.

Finally, insights into existing (distance) communication technologies suggest that emerging touch technologies will not exist in isolation; 'to understand how a given relationship might be shaped by communication technologies, one needs to take into account the way the management of a given relationship will rely on the whole available technoscape' (Licoppe 2004: 135). Inspired by the same literature, we might ask whether 'ambient touching' is as possible as 'ambient dwelling' or viewing, or whether the OSS, for instance, is an example of a new bio-sensing 'connected presence'.

One issue we have not discussed in depth but which is relevant across the above case studies is the way in which our mere engagement with touch technologies may connect us, bring us closer to (or indeed disconnect us from) other people, near, far, living, deceased, and imagined. This is already the case for such 'imagined' digital communities (Appadurai 1990) as health trackers, virtual reality gamers or, more controversially perhaps, users and proponents of sex robots. What will become embodied acts of digital touch may both be felt and observed as such by others, thus becoming meaningful in their own right (cf. our chapters on social norms and wider discourses). Engaging speculatively with these wider relations, connotations and aspirations is part of understanding socio-technical imaginaries of digital touch, as we discuss in Chap. 6.

References

Abrash M (2015) Keynote. Oculus Connect 2. https://www.youtube.com/watch?v=tYwKZDpsjgg. Last access June 2019

Appadurai A (1990) Disjuncture and difference in the global cultural economy. Publ Cult 2:1–24

Baym NK (2015) Personal connections in the digital age. Polity Press, Cambridge

Biocca F, Harms C, Burgoon JK (2003) Toward a more robust theory and measure of social presence: review and suggested criteria. Presence Teleop Virt 12(5):456–480

Candlin F (2010) Art, museums and touch. Manchester University Press, Manchester

Cantó-Milà N, Núñez-Mosteo F, Seebach S (2016) Between reality and imagination, between you and me: emotions and daydreaming in times of electronic communication. New Media Soc 18:2395–2412

Chatterjee H, Noble G (2013) Museums, health and well-being, 1st edn. Routledge, Farnham/Burlington

Cranny-Francis A (2011) Semefulness: a social semiotics of touch. Soc Semiot 21:463–481

Dimmick J, Feaster JC, Ramirez A (2011) The niches of interpersonal media: relationships in time and space. New Media Soc 13:1265–1282

Eid MA, Osman HA (2016) Affective haptics: current research and future directions. IEEE Access 4:26–40

Goffman E (1959) The presentation of self in everyday life. Anchor Books/Random House, New York

Hjorth L, Wilken R, Kay G (2012) Ambient intimacy: a case study of the iPhone, presence, and location-based social media in Shanghai, China. In: Hjorth L, Burgess J, Richardson I (eds) Studying mobile media: cultural technologies, mobile communication, and the iPhone. Routledge, New York, pp 43–62

Huisman G (2017) Social touch technology: a survey of haptic technology for social touch. IEEE Trans Haptics 10:391–408

Jewitt C, Price S (2019) Family touch practices and learning experiences in the museum. Sens Soc 14:221–235

Kim J, Kim H, Tay BK, Muniyandi M, Srinivasan MA, Jordan J, Mortensen J, Oliveira M, Slater M (2004) Transatlantic touch: a study of haptic collaboration over long distance. Presence 13:328–337

Kozel S (1994) Spacemaking: experiences of a virtual body. Available in: http://www.art.net/~dtz/kozel.html (Extended version available In: Dance Theatre Journal 11(3): 46–47). Last access June 2019

Lambert A (2016) Intimacy and social capital on Facebook: beyond the psychological perspective. New Media Soc 18:2559–2575

Leder Mackley K, Jewitt C, Price S (under review) In touch with baby: parenting and bio-sensing as mediated touch

Licoppe C (2004) 'Connected' presence: the emergence of a new repertoire for managing social relationships in a changing communication technoscape. Envir Plann D Soc Space 22(1):135–156

Lupton D (2013) Infant embodiment and interembodiment: a review of sociocultural perspectives. Childhood 20:37–50

Mackenzie D, Wajcman J (1999) The social shaping of technology, 2nd edn. Open University Press, Buckingham/Philadelphia
Madianou M (2016) Ambient co-presence: transnational family practices in polymedia environments. Global Netw 16:183–201
Madianou M, Miller D (2013) Polymedia: towards a new theory of digital media in interpersonal communication. Int J Cult Stud 16:169–187
Madigan J (2010) Analysis: the psychology of immersion in video games. In: Gamasutra: The art and business of making games
O'Hara K, Massimi M, Harper R, Rubens S, Morris J (2014) Everyday dwelling with WhatsApp. In: Proceedings of the 17th ACM conference on computer supported cooperative work and social computing Baltimore, Maryland, USA. ACM, New York, pp 1131–1143
Obrist M, Subramanian S, Gatti E, Long B, Carter T (2015) Emotions mediated through mid-air haptics. In: Proceedings of the 33rd annual ACM conference on human factors in computing systems, CHI '15. ACM, New York, pp 2053–2062
Parisi D (2018) Archaeologies of touch: interfacing with haptics from electricity to computing. University of Minnesota Press, Minneapolis. Kindle Edition
Park YW, Bae SH, Nam TJ (2016) Design for sharing emotional touches during phone calls. Arch Des Res 29:95–106
Paterson M (2006) Feel the presence: technologies of touch and distance. Environ Plann D Soc Space 24:691–708
Pink S, Leder Mackley K, Mitchell V, Wilson GT, Bhamra T (2016) Refiguring digital interventions for energy demand reduction. In: Pink S, Ardevol E, Lanzeni D (eds) Digital materialities: design and anthropology. Bloomsbury, London, pp 79–98
Puig de la Bellacasa M (2009) Touching technologies, touching visions. The reclaiming of sensorial experience and the politics of speculative thinking. Subjectivity 28(1):297–315
Short J, Williams E, Christie B (1976) The social psychology of telecommunications. Wiley, London/New York
Stafford L (2004) Maintaining long-distance and cross-residential relationships. Routledge, Mahwah
Tanaka F, Cicourel A, Movellan JR (2007) Socialization between toddlers and robots at an early childhood education center. Proc Natl Acad Sci 104(46):17954–17958
Thrift N (2000) Afterwords. Environ Plann D Soc Space 18(2):213–255
van Erp J, Toet A (2015) Social touch in human-computer interaction. Front Digit Humanit 2:1–14
Wang J, O'Kane AA, Newhouse N, Sethu-Jones GR, de Barbaro K (2017) Quantified baby: parenting and the use of a baby wearable in the wild. Proc ACM Hum Comput Interact 1(CSCW):108:1–108:19

Chapter 6
Sociotechnical Imaginaries of Digital Touch

Abstract This Chapter explores the potential of the concept of sociotechnical imaginaries for digital touch communication research and design. It defines the social imaginary and discusses how it works to produce and animate shared systems of meaning and belonging that guide and organize the world, in its histories as well as performed visions of desirable futures through advances in science and technology and imagined technological possibilities. The chapter explores the ways in which this concept can be employed as both a design resource, and as a methodological resource. We argue that as new digital touch technologies enter the communicational landscape the setting for interpersonal sociability is/will be reworked. We explore and make legible emerging sociotechnical imaginaries of digital touch, asking how might touch practices be changed through the uses of technology, and how might this shape communication. In particular, the chapter explores the core themes of the body, time, and place in relation to participants' sociotechnical imaginations of digital touch. Turning our attention to the sociotechnical imaginary as a methodological resource, we describe our use of a range of creative, making and bodily touch-based methods to access participants' sociotechnical imaginaries of digital touch and to both explore and re-orientate to the past, present and futures of digital touch communication.

Keywords Sociotechnical imaginary · Digital touch · Touch · Communication · Body · Time · Place · Creative methods · Prototypes · Multimodality · Multisensory

6.1 Introduction

This chapter explores the potential of the concept of sociotechnical imaginaries for digital touch communication research and design. We discuss how this concept can be employed to explore digital touch, as both a design resource, and as a methodological resource. We argue that as new digital touch technologies enter the com-

C. Jewitt et al., *Interdisciplinary Insights for Digital Touch Communication*, Human–Computer Interaction Series,
https://doi.org/10.1007/978-3-030-24564-1_6

municational landscape the setting for interpersonal sociability is/will be reworked. We explore and make legible emerging sociotechnical imaginaries of digital touch, asking how might touch practices be changed through the uses of technology, and how might this shape communication. The core themes of the body, time, and place are discussed in relation to case study participants' sociotechnical imaginations of digital touch. Turning our attention to the sociotechnical imaginary as a methodological resource, we describe our use of a range of creative, making and bodily touch-based methods across the InTouch case studies to access participants' sociotechnical imaginaries of digital touch and to both explore and re-orientate to the past, present and futures of digital touch communication. First, we outline what we mean by the term sociotechnical imaginaries and why it matters for digital touch.

An imaginary describes people's visions, symbols and associated feelings about something. The social imaginary resides in society rather than an individual person's mind and refers to the "common understanding that makes possible common practices and a widely-shared sense of legitimacy" (Taylor 2004: 23). These imaginaries help to produce shared systems of meaning and belonging that guide how people collectively see and organize the world, in its histories as well as its futures (Jasanoff and Kim 2015). The sociotechnical imaginary refers to "collectively held and performed visions of desirable futures…animated by shared understandings of forms of social life and social order attainable through, and supportive of, advances in science and technology" (Jasanoff 2015: 25).

Appadurai (1990) links the social imaginary with the global cultural flow of 'Technoscapes', that is, the ways in which technology promotes cultural interactions. The development and usage of *all* technologies is embedded within and animated by social imaginaries (Herman et al. 2015). While Flichy (2007) argues that there are a range of imagined technological possibilities at the root of a sociotechnical context that warrant investigation, 'not as the initial matrix of a new technology but rather as one of the resources mobilized by the actors to construct a frame of reference'. As this makes clear, social imaginaries serve "as a key ingredient in making social order" (Jasanoff and Kim 2015: 122) and thus have real material outcomes, rather than being ephemeral visions.

The concept of the sociotechnical imaginary has significant theoretical and methodological power for understanding digital touch communication. We use examples from our case studies to illustrate our use of sociotechnical imagination first to explore digital touch to make legible emergent sociotechnical imaginaries of digital touch; and second, to generate new methodological routes towards digital touch futures. InTouch is interested in emerging sociotechnical imaginaries of touch as it is digitally mediated. We ask how the imaginary is articulated across different levels, including that of the individual, which, while less uniform, is always connected to dominant social imaginaries – even if through opposition or resistance to them.

6.2 The Sociotechnical Imaginary as a Design Resource

The sociotechnical imaginary is a key concept, albeit often implicitly, for researchers, engineers, computer scientists and designers working with digital touch. It is used to explore how people make sense of their visions and practices with communication systems, for example, Mansell's *Imagining the Internet* (2012). The imaginations of media and popular culture, particularly the alternate realities of science fiction, are a rich source of inspiration for future digital innovation that is drawn on by engineers, computer scientists, and designers (Finn and Cramer 2014; Shedroff and Noessel 2012). The imagination is also drawn on as a form of critique, "By acting on people's imaginations rather than the material world, critical design aims to challenge how people think about everyday life" (Dunne and Raby 2013: 45). Speculative design has engaged with the imagination (albeit to different extents) to ask provocative questions and disrupt thinking rather than to create design solutions (ibid). Beyond these, sometimes fantastical, futures, however, the imagination pervades the 'everyday' processes of researching and designing digital touch. It weaves through ideation and development (e.g. imagining people's expectations) and the lived social contexts that are evoked through the processes of research and design.

6.3 The Sociotechnical Imaginary as Methodological Resource

We use the sociotechnical imaginary in InTouch as a methodological resource to examine past, present, and future experiences, desires, and fears of touch and remote communication that may shape the evolving digital landscape of touch. It is a useful framing device with which to explore emerging digital touch communication as the majority of digital touch technologies are at an early stage of development, unstable and un-domesticated, in labs rather than 'in the wild'. As a result, observing their everyday use is impracticable or impossible. Further, in addition to the norms of digital touch (see Chap. 4), the potentials for using digital touch to communicate, the forms that this might take, and the contexts of use are in an unsettled state of flux. Highlighting the value of using the socio-technical imaginary of digital touch, to bring the social aspects of digital touch communication to the table of technical development. In our research, we use the concept of the sociotechnical imaginary to frame our exploration of participants' emergent desires, concerns and preoccupations within speculative futures, and to trace the intimate connects of these futures to the present and the past. Exploring case study participants' narratives of continuity and change through this lens enables us to generate a discursive space which "oscillates between imagination and reality" (Kim 2018: 176–7). This has enabled us to "engage directly with the ways in which people's hopes and desires for the future – their sense of self and their passion for how things ought to be – get bound up with the hard stuff of past achievements" (Jasanoff 2015: 32).

The sociotechnical imaginary opens up a research space in which to reflect on and explore touch through attention to emergent potential 'templates for social practice…a map designed to enable some social actions and constrain others' (Herman et al. 2015: 190). This imaginative space enables us to simultaneously look "*into* the future" and "*at* the future", in order to analytically engage with "developments in the present" (Borup et al. 2006: 286). Understanding futures as they unfold is, however, methodologically complex:

> The unprecedented is necessarily unrecognizable. When we encounter something unprecedented, we automatically interpret it through the lenses of familiar categories, thereby rendering invisible precisely that which is unprecedented. …the unprecedented reliably confounds understanding; existing lenses illuminate the familiar, thus obscuring the original by turning the unprecedented into an extension of the past. (Zuboff 2019: 12)

While the boundaries of digital touch are being pushed to new frontiers, our case studies show that the tactile affordances of current technologies combined with the social norms of touch persistently shape the future visions of digital touch. At times these histories actively constrain and limit the visions of designers and potential users. Whilst acknowledging these difficulties, we cautiously wrap the sociotechnical imaginary within our multimodal and multisensorial approach to 'illuminate the role of imagination in the fabrication of social lives' (Appadurai 1990) with respect to digital touch communication.

6.4 Making Legible Emergent Sociotechnical Imaginaries of Digital Touch

As new digital touch technologies enter the communicational landscape, the setting for interpersonal sociability will be reworked. We set out to explore and make legible emerging sociotechnical imaginaries of digital touch; how touch practices might be changed through the use of technology, and how this might shape communication. Alongside the literature, we draw on illustrative examples from the InTouch case studies, notably *Imagining Remote Personal Communication, Designing Digital Touch,* and *Tactile Emoticon.*

In the *Imagining Remote Personal Communication* case study, for example, we used this approach in a series of workshops to engage participants in brainstorming, with the technological probe 'Kissenger', and a rapid prototyping activity to elicit their digital touch imaginaries. The concept of the sociotechnical imaginary framed the analysis of video recordings of the participants' processes of materializing and performing ideas for digital touch for remote personal communication. We analysed the prototypes as imagined touch-interfaces, understanding them as articulating and generating common understandings, and practices of the 'social imaginary' (Taylor, 2004), and providing insight on the participants' cultural values and conventions (Manovich 2001) with respect to touch communication. Across this and other case studies the body, time, and place – as they partly emerged from the data and partly crystallised through our multimodal and multisensorial theoretical lenses – were core to participants' sociotechnical imaginations of digital touch (Fig. 6.1).

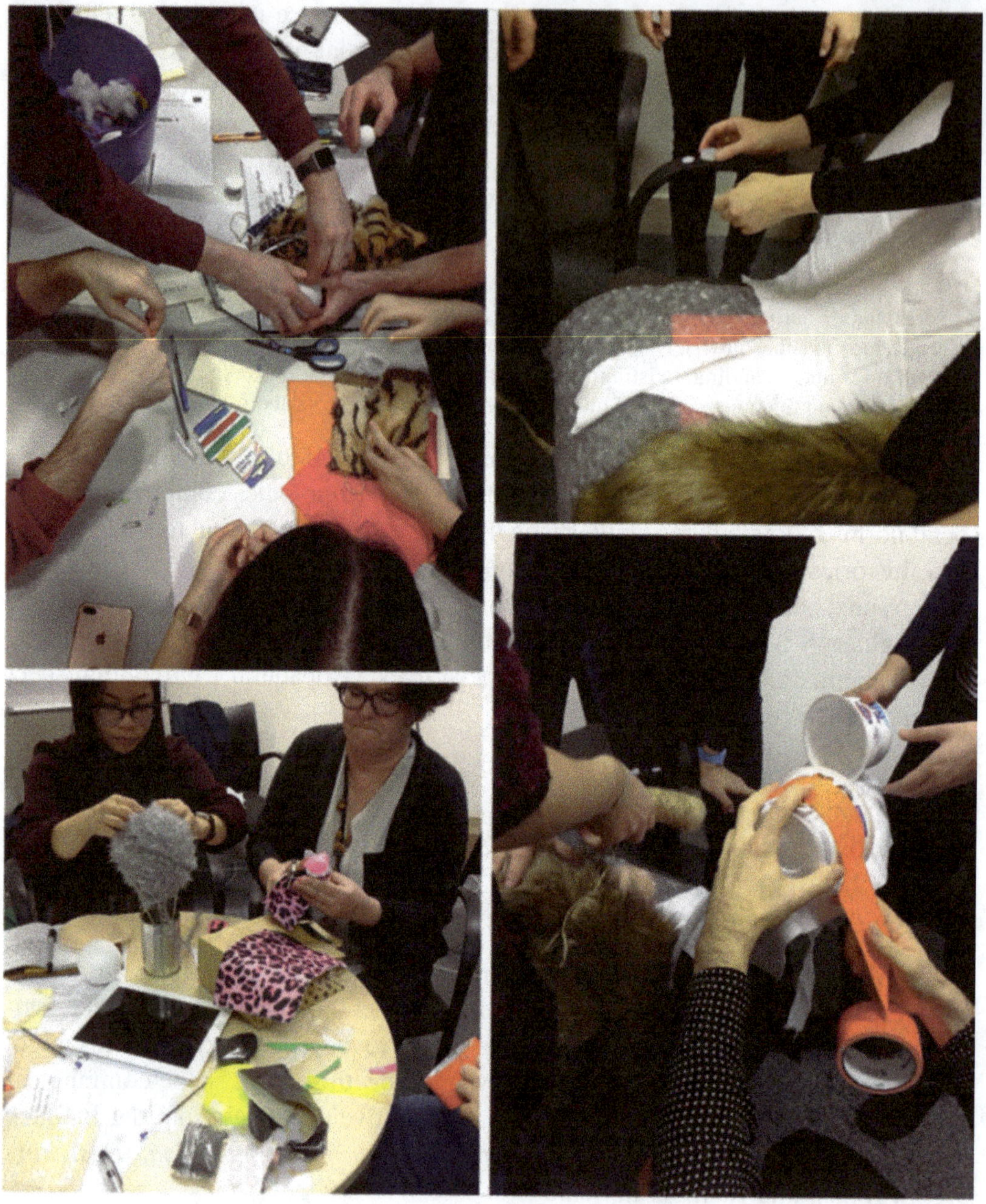

Fig. 6.1 Participants in the Imagining Remote Personal Communication case study engaged in prototyping to elicit their digital touch imaginaries

6.4.1 Body

Imaginations of the body as a location for touch correction and disciplining was made legible through the ways in which participants engaged with a wide range of current touch technologies (bio-sensing, vibro-tactile feedback, the use of air, mid-air haptics) and conjured up new kinds of digital materialities and affordances – extending touch into the realm of the virtual, neuro-telepathy and fictional landscapes of digital touch. As we discussed in Chap. 4, vibration, mobile phones, apps, and wearables were a prominent feature in these imagined landscapes of

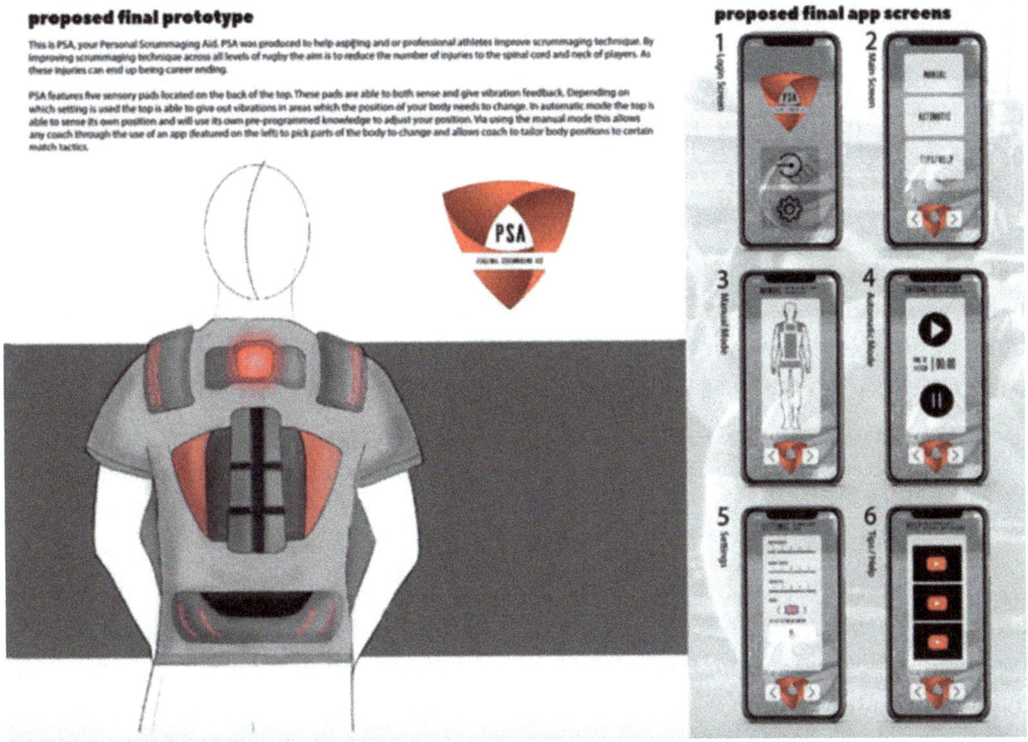

Fig. 6.2 Example of the use of vibration as a form of tactile correction in the *Designing Digital Touch* case study|Personal Scrummaging Aid by Ben Cook: https://issuu.com/bencook11/docs/hd_portfolio (© Ben Cook)

remote touching bodies. While in the *Imagining Remote Personal Communication* case study, vibration was primarily used to convey connection and/or presence, it was extended in the *Designing Digital Touch* case study to also include vibration as a kind of tactile corrective punishment. For instance, many of the students' design concepts imagined the use of digital touch feedback to re-shape the body or a bodily-technique, or the use of a tool through corrective touch via motion sensing feedback, or temperature re-calibration, disciplining the body through touch into an idealized body. For example, a device worn on the user's wrist would vibrate if they spent too long on their phone or to encourage the correct grip of a tool. The ideal normative body (commented on in Chap. 4) that is a fit, available, healthy body, was produced through participants' emergent sociotechnical imaginations of digital touch (Fig. 6.2).

A desire for the borders and boundaries between touching bodies and technologies was made legible in the ways that designers and participants framed digital touch in relation to the body, and for many the social norms that govern where and whose body it is appropriate to touch persist in the realm of the digital (see Chap. 4). This touchy landscape provides the backdrop to the sociotechnical imaginaries of digital touch. The majority of participants in the *Imagining Remote Personal Touch Communication* case study went beyond existing norms to imagine bringing the whole body into their digital touch experiences, a digital amplification or reconfiguration of touch to compensate for the current tactile '*lack*' and '*not enoughness*' of digital communication. The *Sparking Presence* prototype, for instance, placed touch on and in the body to create an always-ready body. A felt '*sparking*' sensation, a '*just-perceptual sense of co-presence*' created a sense of '*belonging*', or '*connected presence*' between the users, and to suggest the potential for a shared body: "*It feels like you are attached, rather than holding something, it's in me, a comfort or an attachment*". Through such imagined embodied interactions, participants developed a variety of tactile and sensory interfaces designed to respond to users who feel "*disconnected*" via the distancing of emotional-sensorial-stripped out technological experiences. In contrast, the *Blocker* prototype situated touch as a sometimes problematic, whole-body sensation:

> Sometimes touch is really painful. What I really wanna communicate is 'don't touch me!' and that is very hard, particularly in a busy city…I'm imagining that all the bad emotions can get filtered off! And the good emotions can get through…so that they can be sensed like where ever your threshold is.

The Blocker prototype expressed a desire to facilitate digital touch through establishing '*boundaries*', '*blocking*' and '*filtering*' it. This and several other prototypes made legible an imaginary of digital touch tied to notions of manipulation, authenticity and a mix of concerns and desires for automation. The potential of digital touch to manipulate – to cut out the 'noise' – was imagined as adding clarity to the messy ambiguities of touching, by offering clear interpretation and the imagined processing of meaning. In the *Tactile Emoticon* case study (see Chap. 1), for example, participants reflecting on their interaction with the device, expected a clarity that does not always exist in physical touch, they wanted the mediated touch to be self-explanatory, suggesting a colour coded feedback system operated by the person receiving the remote digital touch to provide an indication of the message they received. This hints at participants' discourses of fear regarding the ambiguity and misuse of touch communication, and discourses of desire that inform imagined digital touch. Such a functionality would introduce a highly explicit feedback practice within remote digital tactile communication, leading to the emergence of new norms and etiquettes. For instance, decisions on when feedback is required, and what it would mean if feedback remained the same for different types of touch (Fig. 6.3).

6.4.2 Time

Explicitly adding touch to the imagined communicational landscape explored across our case studies made legible debates around societal fears of 'new technologies' – digital privacy and safety, as well as questions of governance of touch, regulation and power. The temporality of touch was central to this imagining. Touch temporalities, the reproduction, traces and records of touch were a key aspect. Participants in the *Designing Digital Touch* and the *Imagining Remote Personal*

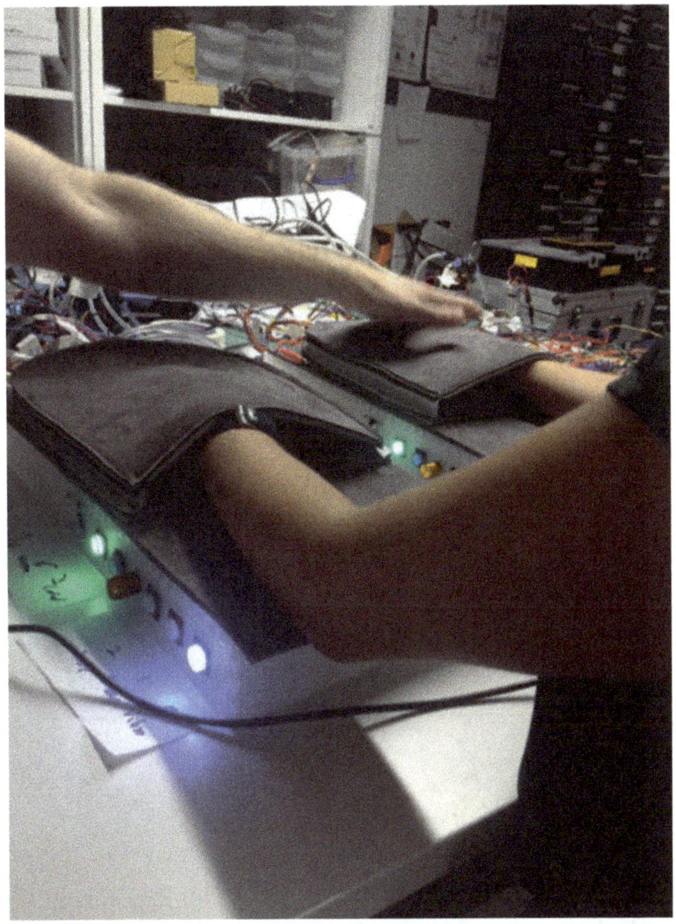

Fig. 6.3 Participants interacting with the *Tactile Emoticon* device

Touch case studies worked with technological, social, and emotional temporal features of touch to structure different touch temporalities and communication experiences through their prototypes. These touch temporalities were shaped through their experiences of different media in terms of communicational "*time-effort*", "*immediacy*", "*spontaneity*" and "*speed*" and managing "*response time*", *and* "*obligations and expectations*". Temporal features included the *duration* of a touch-experience, *social timing* of touch (e.g. a special, every-day or routine time), the a-synchronicity or synchronicity of a sent touch. Prototyping enabled them to explore the practicalities of receiving and responding to a digital touch (e.g. the ability to turn touch on or off), the social time and place for touch ("*not in the street!*") and the communicational consequence of not being available to receive a touch were explored through prototyping (e.g. the potential, and consequences, for scheduling-touch, the inclusion or exclusion of record and replay features – pause, repeat), the storage of touch and timed-filters to manipulate touch (e.g. "*amplify*", "*reduce*", or "*remove*" touch). Many participants focused on the use of touch for time efficiency, others wanted to ameliorate the social impacts of (too) fast communication temporality or to orchestrate touch in relation to shared routine time, others rejected this temporal structuring as '*too staged*', '*practiced*' and feeling '*in-authentic*' and set out to create an '*un-orchestrated immediacy*', with dedicated time for touch communication they designed an element of excitement and anticipation (imagination) of touch into their prototypes. This suggests that, at least for some participants, digital touch has potential to recover time, a form of resistance to the disciplining of the communicative body desired by contemporary industry and capital (Parisi and Farman 2019). In this way, digital touch was imagined as having a potential for a more intimate and sensorial, felt way of being together extending the 'ambient-presence' afforded by long duration skype, resonating with evolving temporal practices of digitally connected or mediated presence (Christensen 2009; Madianou 2016). Through, for example, the conceptualization of connecting through the long-settled touch of domestic intimacy (e.g. the Haptic Chair, Bed-Touch) – drawing on the potentials of touch to secure permanence and the management of the blurry boundaries between absence and presence (Licoppe 2004). These participants conceptualized digital touch, at least for remote personal communication, as having different temporal durations and qualities than digital communication involving visual and audio modes. Digital touch had a longer duration in contrast to the bite size voice message or mobile call, the brevity of a written text or tweet, or the visual flash of snapchat or Instagram. This, together with emplaced and embodied touch, set digital touch apart from contemporary 'anytime, anywhere, anybody' modes of communication.

6.4.3 Place

The Place of digital touch was made legible through the participants' imagination and discussion as key to how technology and communication mutually constitute, organize and structure one another and the practices of digital touch. Participants approached digital touch as more intense, and riskier than other forms of communication. The *Designing Digital Touch* case study explored digital touch in the context of health and well-being, leisure/sport, and generated design scenarios that explored the remote administration of digital touch in a range of public settings. In contrast, the home was the primary imagined space for remote personal touch in the *Imagining Remote Personal Communication* and the *Tactile Emoticon* case studies. Participants reflected on how mobile connectivity reconfigures their spaces of communication to stretch and shrink communicational time and language (e.g. across public and private transport). They associated the 'anywhere, anytime' dimension of mobility to authentic '*in-the-moment-communication*', but the ways that they imagined the time and space of digital touch disrupted this contemporary mantra. As one participant said, "*Where would this happen? Not on the street? It's so personal. I wouldn't feel comfortable. You are walking in the street. I want to sit on the sofa at home and feel this warmth, cos it's like personal. Out of the home –NO!*" In these two case studies, the majority of participants did not include mobility as a key concept for their design of digital touch for remote personal communication, locating digital touch in a domestic and private place: usually the home: a tactile equivalent of the sonic-quiet sought for a spoken conversation appears to be a place where the body is at rest, static with a calm heartbeat, ready to be 'activated'. Three analytical rationales appeared to underpin this domestication of digital touch: touch as intimate and taboo; the '*slower*' temporal quality of touch; and the sense that it requires a "*prepared place*" including a preparing and imagination of the self and the other for communication (Cantó-Milà and Núñez-Mosteo 2016: 2409). This emerging social norm may lessen over time enabling digital touch to come out of the home, changing practices and capacities and giving rise to a need for different kinds of touch awareness and sensitivity in the management of communication.

The sociotechnical imaginaries that Virtual reality (VR) emplace touch in a common virtual space that collapses the distance between the people (users) in physical places, to bring them into connection via a shared tactile experience. Touch takes place in the virtual space and it is digitally transmitted and physically felt in these different locations. It is the type of virtual environment and the affordances – possibilities and constraints of the VR peripherals and the narratives supported by that environment, rather than those of the physical place of the users, that determines the types and norms of touch that are brought into the virtual interaction. Place is often a point of contrast in VR, for example, dystopian science fiction VR environments often juxtapose a polished virtual space with a destructed real-world space. This contrast is designed to demonstrate a sense that the physical does not matter with the physical body positioned as a mere container, emphasised by the body often being imagined as isolated in such VR environments. In contrast, the virtual space is positioned as the one that matters, because it is a shared space which hosts and facilitates co-presence and touch. Furthermore, in these imaginaries the virtual becomes a refuge from the physical or an 'alterity' (a different reality) where different rules, constraints, possibilities and opportunities apply. Users in a virtual world can, depending on the social and technological affordances available to them, reshape their 'bodies', re-fashion who they touch, how, when and in which spaces they touch. These imaginaries demonstrate how the emplacement of touch in a virtual space can accomplish a realistic tactile connection with the physical body, generate questions about the body, physical space, the forms and norms of touch, the boundaries between the physical and the digital as well as the resources which the virtual can bring to touch experience.

Three key cross-cutting themes emerged through the participants' articulations of the sociotechnical imaginaries of digital touch communication outlined above in the form of speculations on touch with regard to the politics of touch, the representation of touch and the ethics of touch. The politics of touch emerged as a theme through participants' (and the researchers') constant debates on touch agency and power: who is being connected via touch, who touches and who is touched, who is untouched, the control of touch, and the types of touch contexts brought into the realm of digital touch (whose touch is important enough to be digitally 'fixed' or enhanced)? The representation of touch and questions of whether (and how) digital touch is mimicking or reconfiguring touch weave through the sociotechnical imaginations of touch made evident by the case studies. They include questions of continuity and change, that is, what forms of touch persist or are lost in the digital remediation of touch, the materiality and affordances of digital touch, its reproduction, traces, recording storage and sharing. The politics and representation of digital touch intersect with the ethics of digital touch, including touch authenticity, privacy and care; themes brought into focus in Chap. 7.

6.5 Generating New Methodological Routes to Imagining Digital Touch Futures

In order to explore the complexity of digital touch, we use a range of methods across the InTouch case studies to engage participants in creative processes, making and bodily touch-activities with themselves, others, materials and objects, that deliberately go beyond the linguistic and the individual. These methods enable us to access participants' sociotechnical imaginaries of digital touch communication and to both explore and re-orientate to its past, present and futures. This has included asking participants to engage in rapid-prototyping of a digital touch communication device, system or environment (discussed above); producing a design-concept video to demonstrate a digital touch user experience; developing or engaging with future scenarios for digital touch; using excerpts from film and fiction as speculative prompts; and interacting with a variety of digital research probes. These methods provide opportunities for participants to reflect on the rich complexities of touch and are particularly adept at accessing participants' sociotechnical imaginaries of digital touch communication. Generating new research spaces for digital touch can help to open up new routes for participants to reimagine touch. We illustrate this approach with reference to the *Tactile Emoticon, Art of Remote Contact* and *Designing Digital Touch* case studies. Though these routes necessarily always tie back to the present and the past of touch, we seek to stretch these threads to explore the new social boundaries of digital touch communication.

The *Tactile Emoticon* case study, (in collaboration with UCL Human Computer Interaction and Neuroscience), provided a specific space to explore the futures of remote personal communication focused on affective or social touch. Through design-workshops and prototype ideation and iteration, participant and designer imaginations of digital touch were used to develop a working prototype of a Tactile Emoticon device. The device is currently being used as a research environment in which participants are given social scenarios which contextualise their exploration of receiving and sending digital touch sensations (as well as an amalgamated digital touch that combines a digitally sent and received touch) (see Chap. 1). This study uses the sociotechnical imaginaries of touch as a design resource, a methodological resource, and a topic of study (Fig. 6.4).

The *Art of Remote Contact* case study 'opens up' a space to explore people's sociotechnical imaginaries of touch through the presentation of artefacts in the Remote Contact exhibition, a collaboration with Interactive Artist Studio Invisible Flock, to provide an exploratory tactile space for touch experiences (see Chap. 1). The interactive artefacts were created to encourage and mediate touch between visitors, to provoke conversations and connections between them, with a broader attention and comment on notions of touch deprivation, loneliness, touch and memory,

Fig. 6.4 Design-workshops and prototype ideation and iteration informed the final Tactile Emoticon Device

and well-being in the context of aging and dementia. Each artefact was described by Invisible Flock, as "an artistic imagining of solutions to issues of isolation, highly tactile installations exploring touch, inviting audiences to use and become part of the evolving data of the artwork" (Fieldnote). They were provocations, not bounded and finished product with a specific design function or purpose, but something that exists through the visitors' interactions. One of the artists described the artefacts as working to digitally create, reconfigure and augment the 'natural interactions that we have' (Fig. 6.5).

The visitors to the exhibition engaged in touch interactions with one another – often with strangers, and with artefacts as objects. The artefacts provoked playful and exploratory ways of touching, including attempts to disrupt the expected ways of touching. This sparked conversation about touch and touching, surfaced questions about touch, pleasant and unpleasant emotions and memories of touching, imaginations of being alone and well-being. It also provoked in-the-moment reactions to touch (e.g. discomfort in holding a stranger's hand). The '*I wanna hold your hand*' artefact, in which visitors held hands, for example, prompted talk of the sensitivity of holding hands, the functions and contexts of doing that, the gendered

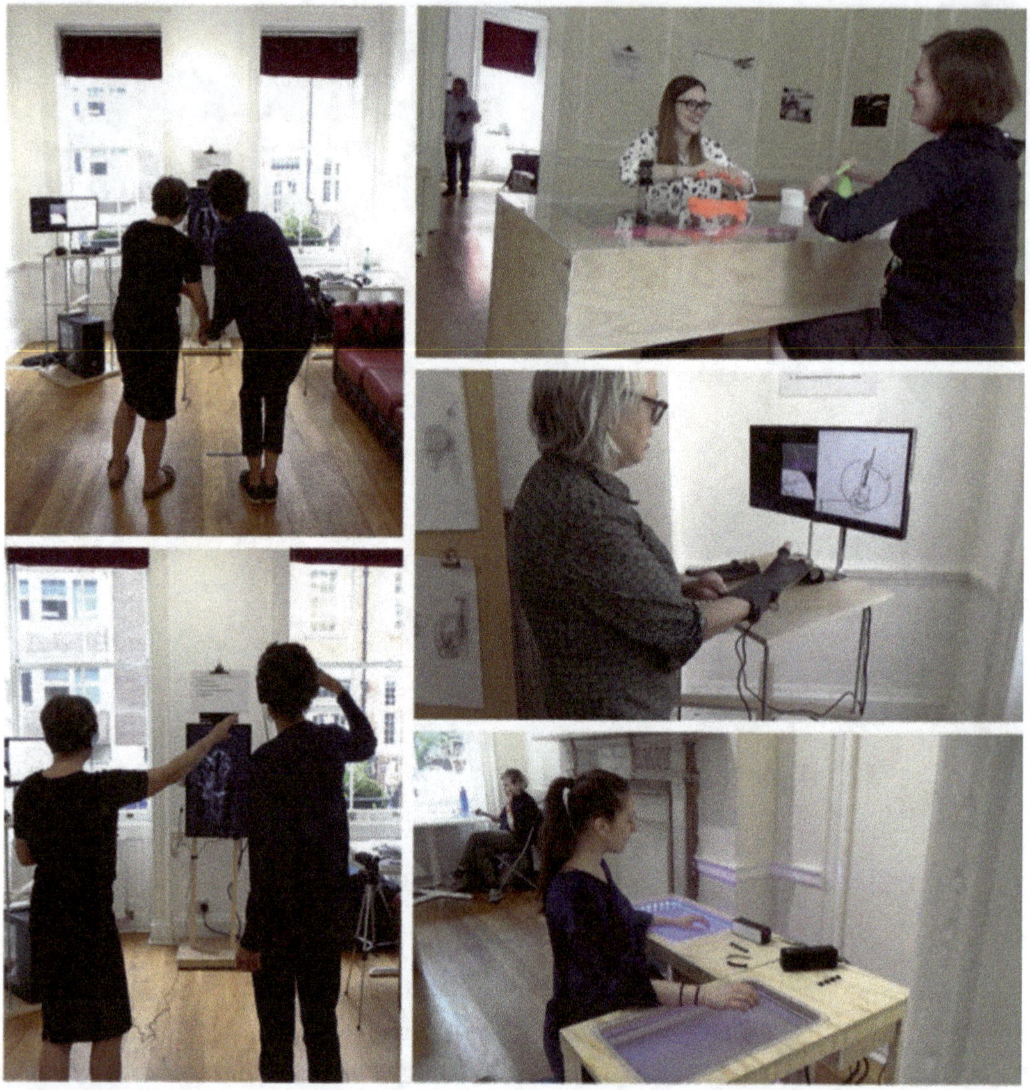

Fig. 6.5 The Art of Remote Contact case study exhibition – Remote Contact, provided an exploratory tactile space for new touch experiences

character of touching, the politicization of touching (or not touching), and individuals' experiences of hand-holding with parents, children, and loved ones, often in the context of family and professional contexts.

The artefacts allowed us to grasp visitors' sociotechnical imaginations of future digital touch, for example, in relation to their expectations, notions of digital touch as activating or controlling communication, the granularity of touch response, the dimensions they expected to feel (e.g. heat, pressure), the types of touch that were meaningful to them in relation to 'feeling connected', as well as imaginations of the relationship they wanted between touch and the digital. Motion Print, a table with a screen embedded in it, two visitors sit opposite one another and knead or manipulate therapy putty which exerts their muscles, each wears a MYO band and the data is fed to an algorithm which changes the visual display on the table-top screen. While interacting with Motion Print, visitors imagined more possibilities for digital touch, for instance the visitor below expressed a desire for more intensive, connected, and responsive touch experiences through the visuality of touch as colour and movement:

> There should be some relationship between colours and movement. Colour communicates something, so the screen should change in response to me. I don't know my heart rate, or temperature or something so that you can create a new image by externalising your internal feelings. [The visitor is associating the 'touch data' with emotion.] That would make you become more aware of yourself, but also how the other person [that you are interacting with via the Motion Print] is making you feel. If it could do those things then the communication between one another would be pleasing and interesting and it would help you think in new ways about how you could transfer what you do intuitively when you touch somebody. How do you make this stuff that is so easy, and familiar and intuitive available for thought? By externalising it, de-familiarising it, and in order to do that, you have to be able to see the connection between what you are doing and the technology.

The exhibition, as the above example suggests, led to imaginations for the representation of touch. One of the artefacts in the '*I wanna hold your hand*' installation was a pair of gloves. The gloves included GPS, pressure sensors, and GSR. When worn by a visitor they generated data that was displayed on the screen in real time. The visitor could press a button and print that representation on an Arduino plotter, and take the print with them. This was, one of the artists, explained, "trying to put a digital layer of friction between these normal interactions, so you make holding hands a little bit more complicated so that maybe you stop and think about it a little bit more and we can begin a new conversation". These visualisations of touch were popular with visitors (many of whom took away their print), and became a site of interpretation and imagination for digital touch. For example, a visitor referred to it as "a map of affection", another wanted to 'make it bigger and paint it!', and another to make it softer:

> They are mechanical, I think for me touch is much softer than what these marks, I wouldn't look at them and associate them with holding someone's hands, they would need to be [*she fluidly moves and squeezes hands*] more organic and softer... do you know what would be great? Is to have a knitting machine instead of a pen, and you could wear it, and someone's touch has made the jumper.

These examples illustrate how the concept of the sociotechnical imaginary can generate new routes to explore digital touch futures, including the materiality of digital touch, social norms and practices, tactile traces, records and representation.

Engaging people in the task of imagining digital touch futures is, however, complex. It can bring forth both utopic and dystopic visions, and it can easily reproduce cliché and stereotypical visions. The challenge of this task is highlighted by the *Designing Digital Touch* case study. In the case study, tracking and observing the students' design process (ideation, experience prototyping, and concept development), highlighted the difficulty of imagining the sociality of digital touch and

Fig. 6.6 The development of the Designing Digital Touch Toolkit. Developed in collaboration with Dr. Val Mitchell and Dr. Garrath T. Wilson, School of Design and Creative Arts, Loughborough University

moving beyond the constraints of dominant digital forms in the current landscape (e.g. mobile phone apps, and on-the-wrist-wearables). In response, we analysed the sticking points that the participants had experienced in the process of imagining and designing digital touch and worked with design colleagues to develop the 'Designing Digital Touch Toolkit' (Fig. 6.6).

The Toolkit is designed to support engagement with the complexities of working with touch. For example, it helps participants to reflect on different types of touch, what touch might mean and feel like in different contexts, as well as bodily sensations and social and cultural boundaries of touch. The Toolkit has three types of cards: 'Filters' – questions to help participants reflect on their own and others' experiences; 'Wild cards' – deliberately abstract prompts for thought or action; and 'Activities' – more structured exercises which require some time. In this way, the Toolkit guides the user by providing new and divergent routes into their imagining of digital touch futures. For instance, a student design project on environmental awareness worked to engage parents and children in gardening and growing plants together towards developing new relationships between people and plants. The length of time a seed takes to germinate was, the student noted, a significant 'pain point', as there is nothing to see and the children become disengaged. Working with the toolkit, they explored ways in which touch could be used to communicate the 'in-pot' activity of the seed to the child through changing temperature, and tactile sensations.

6.6 Conclusion

This chapter has outlined the concept of the sociotechnical imaginary and illustrated its theoretical and methodological potential for understanding digital touch communication as a design resource, a methodological resource, and a topic of study.

The sociotechnical imagination featured as a design resource for the students and participants exploring the futures of digital touch, notably in the *Designing Digital Touch, Imagining Personal Touch Communication,* and the *Tactile Emoticon* case studies. In addition to understanding the sociotechnical imaginaries that circulate among the users and contexts that we are researching and designing for, this chapter makes the case for exploring our own sociotechnical imaginaries, towards an explicit awareness of how they that underpin and drive our research and design of digital touch. Such an awareness can enable us to better articulate the social parameters that underpin our work, in order to understand how our imaginaries 'tacitly' constrain and afford research and design. It can provide a springboard from which to move beyond, extend, or disrupt them.

As a methodological resource, the concept of the sociotechnical imaginary worked to generate new routes to imagining digital touch futures through the making of rapid prototypes of digital touch devices, particularly in the development of the *Remote Contact* exhibition research space, the digital touch experiences we were able to explore via the *Tactile Emoticon* device, and the Designing Digital Touch Toolkit.

As a topic of study, the sociotechnical imaginary enabled us to flesh out the sociality of digital touch communication by making legible emergent imaginaries of digital touch communication, providing critical understanding and insight on digital touch communication futures, and excavating and interrogating the features of sociotechnical imaginaries that 'tacitly' constrain and afford research and design of digital touch. We have discussed how the participants' sociotechnical imaginaries of digital touch communication related to the body, temporality and spatiality and drawn out three key themes that emerged through these articulations and deployments of the sociotechnical imaginary, in the form of speculations on touch with regard to the political economy of touch, the representation of touch and the ethics of touch – a theme taken up in the next chapter.

At a moment where the gap between the science fiction of digital touch communication and reality appears to be quickly narrowing, perhaps the sociotechnical imagination enables us to glimpse some aspects of our potential digital futures, and to engage with thinking what we want from the sociality of digital touch communication. Exploring sociotechnical imaginaries is therefore a vital resource towards a future agenda for the relatively uncharted territory of digital touch.

References

Appadurai A (1990) Disjuncture and difference in the global cultural economy. Public Cult 2(2):1–24

Borup M, Brown N, Konrad K (2006) The sociology of expectations in science and technology. Technol Anal Strateg Manag 18(3–4):285–298

Cantó-Milà N, Núñez-Mosteo F (2016) Between reality and imagination, between you and me: emotions and daydreaming in times of electronic communication. New Media Soc 18(10):2395–2412

Christensen TH (2009) 'Connected presence' in distributed family life. New Media Soc 11(3):433–451

Dunne A, Raby F (2013) Speculative everything. The MIT Press, Cambridge, MA

Finn E, Cramer K (2014) Hieroglyph: stories and visions for a better future. Harper Collins, New York

Flichy P (2007) The internet imaginaire. MIT Press, Cambridge, MA

Herman A, Hadlaw J, Swiss T (2015) Theories of the mobile internet: mobilities, assemblages, materialities, and imaginaries. In: Herman A, Hadlaw J, Swiss T (eds) Theories of the mobile internet. Routledge, New York

Jasanoff S (2015) Future imperfect: science, technology, and the imaginations of modernity. In: Jasanoff S, Kim S (eds) Dreamscapes of modernity. University of Chicago Press, Chicago

Jasanoff S, Kim SH (eds) (2015) Dreamscapes of modernity: sociotechnical imaginaries and the fabrication of power. The University of Chicago Press, Chicago

Kim E (2018) Sociotechnical imaginaries and the globalization of converging technology policy. Sci Cult 27(2):175–197

Licoppe C (2004) 'Connected' presence: the emergence of a new repertoire for managing social relationships in a changing communication technoscape. Environ Plann D Soc Space 22(1):135–156

Madianou M (2016) Ambient co-presence: transnational family practices in polymedia environments. Global Netw 16(2):183–201

Manovich L (2001) The language of new media. The MIT Press, Cambridge, MA

Mansell R (2012) Imagining the internet. Oxford University Press, Oxford

Parisi D, Farman J (2019) Tactile temporalities: the impossible promise of increasing efficiency and eliminating delay through haptic media. Converg Int J Res New Media Technol 25:40–59. https://doi.org/10.1177/1354856518814681

Shedroff N, Noessel C (2012) Make it so: interaction design lessons from science fiction. Rosenfeld Media, Brooklyn

Taylor C (2004) Modern social imaginaries. Duke University Press, Durham

Zuboff S (2019) The age of surveillance captialism. Public Affairs, Hachette Books, New York

Chapter 7
Digital Touch Ethics and Values

Abstract This chapter examines key ethical considerations and challenges of designing and researching touch technologies, with a focus on incorporating ethical touch sensitivities and values into digital touch communication. We discuss the difficulty of researching and designing ethically in the context of an emerging technological landscape, as reflected in wider HCI ethics debate. The chapter then explores the central role of the human body as site for digital touch communication, before focusing on key challenges around trust, control, consent, and tactile data. In line with preceding chapters, we argue that digital touch practices are part of, and impact on, wider social relations and communications. The kinds of touch practices and relations designed *into* touch technologies bring with them implications for power relations and social cohesion, and it is these wider processes that digital touch design is able to – at least in parts – anticipate and shape. We close with a summary of key points and their implications for research and design.

Keywords Ethics · Values · Body · Machine · Consent · Control · Robotic touch · Remote touch · Privacy · Trust

7.1 Introduction

This chapter examines key ethical considerations and challenges of designing and researching touch technologies, with a focus on incorporating ethical touch sensitivities and values into digital touch communication. We propose what 'ethical touch' and 'ethical touch technologies' can mean, and why they matter. Some of the ethical challenges we discuss are more widely true for HCI research and design around emerging, interactive and connected technologies, including questions of consent, agency, harm, ownership, privacy and trust (Waycott et al. 2016). Here, we draw out how touch is 'special', firstly, because it is so directly related to our bodies – as part of our (human) identities and selfhood, as a place where experience and

C. Jewitt et al., *Interdisciplinary Insights for Digital Touch Communication*, Human–Computer Interaction Series,
https://doi.org/10.1007/978-3-030-24564-1_7

the social are felt and articulated. And, secondly, as the preceding chapters have demonstrated, touch practices are part of, and impact on, wider social relations and communications. The kinds of touch practices and relations designed *into* touch technologies bring with them implications for power relations and social cohesion, and it is these wider processes that digital touch design is able to – at least in parts – anticipate and shape.

The themes we address in this chapter derive from the literature, InTouch case studies, and our CHI 2018 workshop, 'Reshaping Touch Communication: An Interdisciplinary Research Agenda' (Price et al. 2018). We refer to ethics and values in both touch technology research and design, acknowledging how these are often intertwined in practice. We begin by situating touch in relation to HCI scholars' ongoing introspection of ethical conduct in light of changing technological and methodological landscapes.

7.2 What Is Ethical Touch?

Questions of ethics are intrinsically bound up with notions of what it means to be human, considerations of good and bad, right and wrong. Ethics is chiefly about preventing harm, with some ethical frameworks weighing up the rights of the individual versus achieving a greater good (Bonde et al. 2016): the power of touch places it at the heart of such questions. Yet, just as social norms change (Chap. 4), what touch is considered harmful within a given community might shift in light of scientific and technological advances, changing methodologies, and social and cultural sensitivities to touch (e.g. gender); in other words, in response to the trajectories of harm as they are experienced, anticipated and made relevant through history.

Much of the literature on unmediated touch makes distinctions between good, bad and absent touch (e.g. Green 2016). On close inspection, these categories are neither self-explanatory nor stable. Absent touch tends to be seen as problematic, partly because a certain 'touch literacy' is required to be able to distinguish between good and bad touch, and these vary across culture. It might result in instances of 'bad' touch, for instance when individuals' 'touch hunger' leads them to search for touch in 'inappropriate or dangerous situations' (Green 2016: 775; Field 2001), when they touch where they should not, or when they misinterpret sexual for platonic touch, a boundary which is often deliberately blurred by child sex abusers and other sexual harassers (Conte et al. 1989, in Green 2016: 774). On the other hand, absent touch might be a welcome relief to people who are either overly sensitive to touch (e.g. through medical conditions) or who feel otherwise protective of their body boundaries, perhaps but not exclusively because of previous instances of unwanted touch.

Examples of 'bad' touch include sexual, and other forms of physical, violence (Green 2016), whereas 'good' touch is generally considered to be the kind of touch that brings physiological, psychological and social benefits. At the same time, violence arguably needs to *violate* to be considered bad, that is, for instance happen against a person's will. Thus, while it might not make sense to base one's touch ethics on categories of 'good' or 'bad' touch, a slightly more helpful (though still imperfect) definition is the distinction between 'welcome' and 'unwelcome' touch. Even so, consent is only part of touch ethics. What might be experienced as unwelcome touch – being restrained by one's parent – can also prevent harm. Conversely, what seems to be welcome touch – affection shown by an adult – may have more sinister undertones or change in light of additional information, such as intent. As such, it matters who touches whom, in what context, with what intention, and to what (felt) consequence. Children are not the only 'vulnerable' members of society here; arguably, anyone can feel manipulated, exploited or violated through touch, depending on what they know and comprehend about the circumstances of touch – and their own power and agency – at any given moment.

These issues are differently complex when it comes to mediated or digital touch. What does informed consent look like in a digital context? We need to clarify how to ensure individuals' agency and control, and how to bring measures of authenticity and transparency to a digital touch moment. Given the above nuances of touch, the ability of a machine to decide between welcome and unwelcome touch and the contexts where that would be appropriate are brought into question. What might it mean for human touch to be 'replaced' by machine touch? The introduction of digital interfaces and algorithms, along with the notion of the machine that touches or mediates touch, bring with it wider questions of the touch sensations, experiences and relations we design for. If it is important to prevent oppressive or abusive forms of digital touch, how do we recognise the latter? What might be the benefits of enabling boundary setting and testing? One of the questions we ask is whether touch should be put to the forefront of design, so as to enable people to reflect and talk about it (Green 2016), or whether design might allow for incidental, hidden or covert touches, as long as they serve a fair purpose (for whom?).

The difficulty of defining ethical touch and devising set guidelines for designing and researching touch technologies is reflected in recent debates on design ethics and values in HCI more generally. We particularly note two trends. First, HCI scholars have outlined the challenges of negotiating universal values and human rights, as they make their way into relatively static and anticipatory ethics guidelines, with the *ad-hoc* ethical issues that arise during a research or design process that increasingly involves more ethnographically inspired, participatory and exploratory approaches (cf. Munteanu et al.'s 'situational' (2015) and Frauenberger et al.'s 'in-action' ethics (2017)). Second, whose values and ethics matter has been a useful but contested focus in a range of design approaches that seek to go beyond questions of functionality to put social implications and ethics at the centre of the design process; namely, participatory design (with its focus on democracy and empowerment), feminist HCI (providing multiple perspectives and a voice to the 'underrepresented', e.g. Bardzell and Bardzell 2011; Muller 2011) and value-sensitive design (VSD, which seeks a systematic approach to reflecting on and accounting for the values and 'desires' of different stakeholders, including designers themselves, Friedman et al. 2008; Winkler and Spiekermann 2018).

These movements, though not free from criticism (Jacobs and Huldtgren 2018), provide useful reading for considering touch ethics and sensitivities, with their focus on reflexivity, responsiveness, diversity and inclusion. In this chapter, we also move beyond immediate interaction contexts to bring into focus some of the wider social (and sensory) meanings and consequences of digital touch. We begin with a key component, its relationship to the human body or, rather, human bodies.

7.3 Touch, Body and 'Machine'

Touch is personal because it involves our bodies – how we know them, how we feel and experience them, and how they encounter other bodies, objects and environments. In mapping the landscape of digital touch, the InTouch project has located touch and, with it, the body in relation to a range of technologies and interfaces. In Chap. 3, we categorised touch technologies according to whether they entailed human-human, human-robot or human-object touch communication. We can also think of touch technologies as implicating or relating to the body in at least one of three ways: as the body interacting with technologies through touch; as technologies becoming part of or augmenting the body; or as technology playing the role of a mediator between our body and the world, including other bodies. These categories are not discrete. When technology plays the role of the mediator, for instance, the very materiality of the interface might bring object interaction into focus (Chap. 5). Likewise, a device that might 'augment' the body, such as an extraskeleton or prosthesis, still mediates between body and environment. As loose categories, however, they allow us to *follow* and explore what forms of touch and bodies (or body parts) are at stake across instances of touch interaction, and beyond. This involves following touch as it is transformed and transforming, as it changes in its meaning and materiality, at the same time as acknowledging bodies as dynamic, multifaceted, physiological and social, and as differently shaped and situated through touch.

7.3.1 Touching Bodies

A key question is what happens to the body, or bodies, at the introduction of digital touch technologies. With a view to supporting bodies and enhancing users' quality of life, some touch technologies actively train, 'realign', shape or stimulate bodies for medical or rehabilitative purposes. Spinal electrical stimulation allows people with Parkinson's Disease to walk (Barzallo et al. 2019); sensory-equipped prosthetics can enable a new sense of touch or feeling (Sun et al. 2018); extraskeletons can aid rehabilitation. In terms of interacting with digital touch interfaces, it is possible to speak of a subtler disciplining of the body into new ways of moving and touching, which might have wider physiological, sensorial and social consequences (e.g. Elo 2012; Parisi 2008). Elo (2012: n.p.) speaks of the 'digital finger' being handed 'the status of a switch' (and, increasingly, 'dragging the body along'), by putting things in reach and changing our bodily and imaginary perception of touch agency and immediacy (Chap. 5). His discussion of technological feedback, as means to demarcate boundaries and regulate touch, highlights the subtle training of sensory skills and expectations. This was evident during InTouch's *The Art of Remote Contact* case study when exhibition visitors tried to make sense of visual and auditory representations of touch as directly linked to their own touches and movements; however, the artistic provocations were more ambiguous and often challenged a direct 1-2-1 relationship of touch and reaction. Bodily feedback along particular digital-material parameters was key in students' imagination of digital touch concepts during the *Designing Digital Touch* case study; here, bodies were nudged into specific positions and kinds of movements, and bodily feelings, states and symptoms were reinterpreted through numbers, vibrations, and emotion displays. Although Elo (2012) critiques some feedback's haptocentrism, certain touch technologies arguably require the accurate representation of unmediated touch, for instance in the context of remote surgical interventions where medical professionals' bodies are most actively trained to *feel* and manipulate interfaces in specific ways (see also O'Neill 2017, on the historical disciplining of doctor-patient touch interaction through the sphygmograph (a mechanical device used to measure blood pressure in the mid-nineteenth century). At an extreme, haptic technologies such as the Teslasuit have the potential to manipulate bodies by activating muscle groups to result in involuntary movements (Savvides 2018). Differently so, and going beyond the felt intricacies or affordances of touch interfaces, the Owlet Smart Sock disciplined babies and parents' bodies by positioning them as static (a moving baby interfered with sensor readings) and geographically separated. In our case study, parents moreover used the mobile app as a sensory extension of touch, giving meaning to sensory readings in a way that allowed them to reinterpret their babies' bodies, partly in relation to their own (Leder Mackley et al. under review). Determining the ethics of touch requires us to ask, then, what kinds of touches, movements, mobilities and socialities are inscribed in touch interfaces and wider user experiences.

At an extreme end, touch technologies have the potential for a sensory or haptic remapping of the body, akin to the kinds of 'body hacking' that are already possible through surgical intervention (e.g. Overgoor Max et al. 2006). Drawing on Rheingold's early 90s visions of telesex, Parisi quotes it might 'eventually be possible "to map your genital effectors to your manual sensors and have direct genital contact by shaking hands," [Rheingold 1991: 352] resulting in the transformation of social touch"' (Parisi 2018). Rheingold saw in cybersex a phenomenon of disembodiment between 'the ultimate sexual revolution', the possibility of experiencing deep multisensorial communion without the risk of pregnancy or sexually transmitted disease, and a first step towards 'abandoning our bodies' (Rheingold 1991: 352). It is significant to note that his vision of technologically mediated safe sex at the apparent expense of fleshly communion (beyond one's own body) emerged during the HIV and AIDS pandemic, a time at which social fears of bodies and bodily fluids, sex and risk were particularly heightened. Teledildonics, technology for remote sex that can communicate tactile sensations over a data link between the participants, has fostered online communities and a number of commercial markets (including webcam sex work). However, some of Rheingold's ideas remain in the realm of the imagined, the forms of sensory remapping that are perhaps most closely aligned with his visions are body hacking practices that involve surgical implants to experience sensations (usually vibration), based on magnetic or digitally mediated inputs (see Chap. 3. Notions of cyborgs are actively entertained through the very reconstitution of the human body as part machine. Moreover, it is possible for technology to play a mediating and, thus, remapping role in augmented/virtual reality or other forms of remote touch communication. This might include changing the location of where on the body touch is received, translating strokes into tickles or punches, or amalgamating touch messages, as in the *Tactile Emoticon* case study (see Sect. 7.4 for issues around trust and control). Of course, the latter still worked within the technical constraints of representing touch through heat, pressure and vibration. This was, on the one hand, a communicatively frustrating restriction. On the other hand, participants seemed to develop new embodied ways of making sense of touch, for instance by working out communication patterns or distinguishing between seemingly identical machines based on their 'feel'. Whether the abstraction of 'human' into 'machine' touch serves a safeguarding purpose is questionable in light of participants' comments on the power of imagined, affective and intended dimensions of mediated touch, an issue that is reflected differently in Kozel's (2007) writing on the virtual-interactive performance piece, 'Telematic Dreaming'. 'The mechanization or computerization of human experience', she writes, 'is generally thought to diminish the physical and emotional sides of life, yet in the virtual world of Telematic Dreaming questions of privacy, intimacy and identity were central' (Kozel 2007: 94; see also Sect. 7.4). The above raises related questions of what is lost or added by the machine's representation of touch. We need to consider what elements of human touch we choose (or need) to digitize. Is touch diminished by being stripped of its uniqueness and individuality, or is there virtue in 'flattening' personal touch into a thing, for instance when it comes to the recording and sharing of machine-mediated touch? The question is not only what happens to bodies but also to human touch at the introduction of digital touch technologies.

7.3.2 *Human Touch*

Human touch is at once positively infused as essential to being human (not to be replaced by a machine), and yet a complicated category in itself which is steeped in social norms and partly requires regulation. Some of the discourses the *In Touch with Baby* case study responded to were, the perceived loss of human touch (and related bonding and affection) and the sensory de-skilling implicated in bio-sensing technology replacing the parent's hand on the child's chest or forehead. While, in the context of our study, unmediated touch continued to play a key role and the device's relatively short lifespan of 18 months puts doubt over the transformation of parents' sensory skillsets, the OSS-enabled new insights into babies' bodies beg the question of whether the device paves the way for similar bio-sensing technologies to eventually saturate a market for all age groups (e.g. toddler and primary school children Fitbits), thus normalising the 'hands-off' hands-on approach. Implications go beyond individual interaction contexts to include how babies' bodies fit into medical and other ideological notions of norms (as regards healthy heart rates or sleeping patterns, cf. Lupton and Williamson 2017), plus related issues of privacy and surveillance (see Sects. 7.3.3 and 7.4).

For some, digital technologies provide a solution to the kinds of problems that arise from unmediated touch. Not only might they enhance human touch in extending its reach, perfecting it as a skill, or enabling new forms of knowing. It might also be possible to teach 'good touch' (although see the limited success of historical attempts to use tactile approaches to induce 'corporeal discipline' Classen 2005, 262), or enable kinds of touch that are at odds with societal touch regimes, in a safe environment, thus preventing 'actual' harm. Two controversial examples are the use of child robots for the 'therapeutic' treatment of pedophilia (Behrendt 2018), and sexbots more generally to reduce human sexual exploitation (prostitution) and harassment. Arnold and Scheutz (2017) articulate a key concern, that '[t]he touch between a person and a robot [...] carries with it the implicit connection to human-human or other forms of touch – how that person will want to touch and be touched in the rest of his or her daily life, and how his or her touching and being touched features for better or worse within a community at large' (2017: 84). Moreover, there are concerns about the mistreatment of robots themselves which, as Whitby reminds us, 'can be aggravated by the provision of anthropomorphic interfaces (De Angeli et al., 2006) or by placing the robot into an intimate setting (Fogg and Tseng 1999)' (Whitby 2008: 327). Besides a general sense of human deprivation linked to any form of abuse (of sentinent, non-sentinent or semi-sentinent beings), a central fear is that if someone abuses human-like artefacts, they are more likely to abuse humans, too. Whitby's solutions include providing guidance on a list of unacceptable activities, such as 'the use of robots in paraphilic sexual activities and purely as the victims of violence' (ibid: 330). Arnold and Scheutz (2017), writing of 'tactile ethics' for soft robotics in social companion or care contexts, suggest that '[f]eeling the touch of others [should be] a robotic conduit for the larger purposes of the system's designers and implementers (therapeutic, companionship, education, etc.). There should be no suggestion, however implicit, that the robot suffers or enjoys the tactile feedback' (2017: 84). In other words, robot touch should be entirely functional as appropriate to the social context (ibid: 85). However, questions of functionality are relative in the context of sex robots, where advances in smart skin technologies mean that robots can feel where on the body they are touched, at what intensity, and by whom (Sheila Media 2018).

Many complexities of human-robot touch and human-machine bodies go beyond the scope of this chapter (see Devlin, 2018; Dix, 2008 for a fuller account). Van Erp and Toet (2013), who foresee that 'over the coming years social agents will increasingly use touch as affective communication channels' (2013: 780), have set out initial guidelines for social agents and robots that can touch, including not hurting users themselves (see also ISO 2009). Crucially, more research is needed to fully understand social and psychological implications of human-robot touch interaction. 'Imagining' vulnerable user groups (in Whitby's case, 'children, or those with known psychiatric disorders' (Whitby 2008: 330)) gives rise to the sorts of moral panics that have historically been attached to a range of new media and technologies, some of which are now considered benign (Drotner 1999). For some of the participants in the *Imagining Remote Personal Touch* case study, the use of the Kissenger brought with it connotations of human-machine interaction, which ranged from the feeling of kissing a massage chair to associations with sex robots. In order to ensure ethical digital touch, future research and design needs to engage with these associations and connotations, in terms of their sensory and social meanings and implications.

7.3.3 Whose Bodies?

The social and moral objections towards human-like robots in certain contexts of human-machine touch interaction bring to the fore an area often neglected in HCI design, that is, the power of representation. Not only does it matter whether robots are human-like *per se*. As Devlin (2018) argues, the kinds of robotic bodies currently designed for sexual interaction are often 'crude' and 'hypersexualized' representations of women, which arguably hold them to 'unrealistic expectations of beauty and shape' (Devlin 2018: 219) and portray visions of touch behaviour and obedience that objectify and disempower the humans they model. Importantly, the question is not only one of behavioural or attitudinal effects, although these require systematic and evidence-based scrutiny. It is also one of wider social meanings; we need to consider what the existence of such robotic representations might mean to women and children's sense of safety and self-worth, and to their understanding of proper and improper touch. While some have called for a ban on sex robots (Richardson 2016; the country-specific legality of child robots illustrates the need for global considerations of digital touch), Devlin has argued for a rethinking of sexbots as 'things', machines or toys, which can take on any number of non-human-like features, sensations and touches (Devlin 2018). Representation is a key ethical dimension to this debate, which speaks to design decisions as to whether to mimic or reconfigure human touch, skin and bodies, as well as the social norms and practices these are embedded within.

Linked to and transcending issues of representation, there are ethical considerations around the kinds of users we imagine when designing touch technologies. As we discussed in Chap. 4, the ways in which touch becomes gendered requires us to attend to the gendered ways in which technologies empower or constrain different members of society. This includes ascribing values to technology that 'encourage progressive attitudes towards gender roles, especially towards feminine values' (cf. 'gender-sensitive design', Rode 2011: 299) Rode's writing on gender as continually socially produced and non-binary is important in light of static and essentialist approaches to gender, moving towards incorporating more inclusivity, diversity and reflexivity in design. Aside from gender, there are other socially constructed or infused categories, such as race (Benjamin 2019), age and disability, that require reflection on the kinds of implicit bias we might bring to touch design.

Importantly, and bearing in mind the complex relationship between physical attributes and social categories, this also extends to the kinds of 'bodies' we design for, and to what end. Noting the dearth of social and ethical research on the meanings and implications of extraskeletons, Sadowski (2014) considers the ambition of enhancing and fixing 'the "impaired" or "disabled" body, so that it fits into societal conceptions of what it means to be "able-bodied"' as working within and enforcing 'structures of ableism and privilege' (Sadowski 2014: 217). In shaping touch technologies and, through them, our bodies, it is thus important to consider what concepts of 'normal' we work with. Likewise, our research has highlighted differences in how people experienced their bodies and, thus, perceived and responded to touch, in terms of medical conditions or sensory preferences (e.g. Chaps. 5 and 6). Other questions are more straightforwardly about devices' sizes, weight and usability, for instance the types of bodies that fit into haptic suits or VR headsets. As per VWVR vision statement notes, 'VR headsets and Sub-packs fit poorly onto female bodies, smaller bodies and cannot accommodate afro hair – a clear indication of who, at the moment, the VR industry's "standard" user is' (VWVR 2018: 9).

The above demonstrate that design needs to reflect on how and whose bodies are implicated in digital touch. In the following we elaborate on what else is at play in the mediation, replication, fragmentation and broadcasting of human (and machine) touch.

7.4 Consent, Trust and Control

Friedman et al. (2008: 69f) list privacy, ownership, physical welfare, freedom from bias, universal usability, autonomy, informed consent and trust as some of the enduring human values guiding value-sensitive design. Here, we reflect in more detail on the ethical specificities and opportunities of digital touch in relation to three interrelated concepts: consent, trust and control. Whilst issues of consent are complex in unmediated touch, these are amplified in contexts in which, firstly, touch does not have to be synchronous, reciprocal or bidirectional and, secondly, touch locations can be moved and sensations transformed, either through mediating technologies or through the actions of touch 'senders' and 'receivers' themselves. In our research, these issues became most apparent in two technological domains, remote personal touch communication and virtual touch (in some cases a sub-section of remote communication). Parisi's (2018) aforementioned handshake becoming something else in digitally mediated contexts resonated with participants' concerns over the possible 'improper' uses of, for instance, the Touch Cape in the *Imagining Remote Personal Touch* case study (a digital cape for remote touch designed to be worn over the shoulders). The relative agency of touch 'receivers' to re-direct the location of touch is not new; an innocent kiss on the cheek can inadvertently or purposefully result in a more intimate kiss on the mouth. Although it is not always possible to mutually shape unmediated touch moments, there is perhaps less opportunity to do so in digital context, and more room for manipulating and concealing the ultimate location, direction or sensation of touch. Likewise, remote and virtual communication may obscure the identity of who is touching or being touched. In the case of our prototyping workshops, participants envisaged systems of visual or auditory authentication; advances in smart skin technology may further utilise the properties of touch for purposes of identification (whilst also raising questions of privacy, see Sect. 7.5).

In the context of virtual touch, some of the considerations of authenticity and trust include whether touch makes avatars believable, and also the extent to which virtual touch needs to be 'physical' (rather than auditory or visual) to be effective in this way (cf. Botvinick and Cohen, 1998). As Parisi, quoted by caddy (2019: n.p.), argues, "even if the reproduction of touch falls short of fully synthesizing the full range of tactile sensations, [...] low-definition can be emotionally meaningful." Believable virtual touch may provide new senses of closeness in social VR (Chap. 5) or, alternatively, enable moments of transgression to feel 'more real' – whether this is experienced as positive or not. Kozel's (2007) writing on 'Telematic Dreaming' suggests that trust is not a static concept that can be easily designed *into* virtual environments, but one that is actively negotiated within specific virtual encounters. She speaks of the sense of 'openness and trust' that lay the foundation for a kind of immersion and connection (our words) that rendered 'the distinction between which bodies were real and which were virtual [...] irrelevant' (2007: 94). 'Little electronic shocks' would pass through her body in response to caressing virtual touch (ibid). Where trust was betrayed, as in a number of violent encounters, the amount to which she felt 'touched' (that is, her body physically reacted despite the absence of physical contact) depended on the severity of the virtual violence, with extreme violence leading her to disassociate herself from her physical body 'in an involuntary act of self-preservation' (ibid: 97).

Digital touch does not only raise questions of trust in the relationship between people but also in the reliability, security and safety of the machines and systems that mediate touch (cf. Friedman et al. 2008). The mediation, recording and broadcasting (sharing) of touch bring issues of agency, control and ownership into focus, both at the initial moment of touch interaction and across time. Just as we proposed following touch (and bodies) through different moments of touch interaction and beyond, we might also consider how agency and control travel across instances of digital touch. Within the context of the *Imagining Remote Personal Touch* case study, participants' addition of buttons to their prototype remote touch devices to turn touch on or off (or record it) sought to place agency and control with users and, specifically, recipients of touch (Jewitt et al. 2020). Other participants designed prototypes that included more or less adjustable touch blockers, and yet others diffused touch through a sense of ambient presence, rather than direct physical contact, although the details of agency in negotiating ambient touch were unclear. The question of how much agency and control is given to the technological mediator is a matter for the ethical design of digital touch – be this the machine or, by extension, its designers or owners – and how easily touch might be intercepted or hacked. Technological devices like Tjacket (formerly Huggy Pajama, Teh et al. 2009) function along normative conceptions of how a person might want/need to be held or touched. At a more extreme end of the spectrum, we might ask if and how mediators should regulate and 'police' touch, that is, prevent brutal or improper digital touch.

Who controls (and owns) touch recordings or memories is partly a question of agency and transparency in 'tactile data' management and also, again, partly of the extent to which touch might be abstracted or personally identifiable through digital reproduction and mediation. Will the touch of one's child – e.g. a baby's first kiss – become a tangible, sharable artefact and, if so, how might digital-mechanical reproduction disguise or attribute the uniqueness of the baby's touch? If someone engages in and records inappropriate or illegal touch, what stops them from sharing these touches with others?

Two other areas of control are worth considering. First, in relation to extraskeletons, Sadowski (2014) raises the question of who controls access to touch technologies, giving the example of definitions – e.g. the difference between body enhancement and rehabilitative aid – as impacting on health insurance payments. Second, Cranny-Francis (2011: 472) highlights how users might find themselves to be mere nodes in digital-technological assemblages 'over which control is distributed' – between soldiers, medical and command staff, in the case of technologically-enhanced battle suits, or between employees and employers, in the case of bio-metric monitoring of employees' stress levels and productivity. 'In these examples', Cranny-Francis writes, 'the "being with" or engagement enabled by the touch (of the uniform) incorporates the wearer into a network that is outside her/his control' Cranny-Francis 2011: 472). The latter leads us to questions over the forms of tactile data touch technologies enable, how these are used and represented, and to what purpose.

7.5 A Note on Study Ethics

In her reflections on the 'anthropologist as toucher', Blake (2011) describes how her attempts to keep a professional, unintrusive distance from the ontology children whose experiences she studied were superseded by the children's requests for emotional support, including affective touch. Rather than resisting the children's 'tactile demands' (2011: 10), Blake came to see these encounters as essential to her ethnographic understanding and position in the field, alerting her to the importance of skin and body in ontology experiences. She advocates employing one's (touch) influence as a 'tool for exploring and satisfying our ethical responsibilities in the field' (ibid: 11).

In our own studies, we found touch equally inescapable and indeed a necessary part of researching touch technologies. Rather than avoiding or ignoring it, we sought to be attentive to participants and colleagues' touch sensitivities, some of which emerged in unexpected ways. Key considerations have included the safeguarding of participants and colleagues during touch-based research activities; introducing different levels of (and an ongoing dialogue about) consent; and understanding and negotiating tactile data protection with stakeholders.

Touch-based activities chiefly happened during research workshops, where we introduced ground rules of touching with consent, as well as during the Remote Contact exhibition. Although the latter touch experiences were not designed by us, we were still complicit in instigating them as part of research encounters. There was a sense that touch in the exhibition space was an unexpectedly 'touching' experience, precisely because it brought visitors into the context of experiencing dementia in new, and sometimes personal ways. One participant, for example, who suffered from anxiety, to us, invisible condition, excessive sweating, shared with us her anxiety over holding hands with a stranger in the Kinect exhibit. InTouch consistently prompts people (e.g. colleagues at conferences, research participants) to share personal histories and stories of touch, notably their family experiences and early childhood memories of touch, touch aversions, and their intercultural experiences and faux-pas. We have an evolving sense, which we need to investigate further, that people may be more skilled at self-censoring visual materials than they are in relation to touch. In response, to manage this we have at times used different levels of consent for different research stages or contexts. A pilot workshop for our *Imagining Remote Personal Touch* case study alerted us to the difference between being video-recorded during rapid prototyping and whilst testing an existing prototype, the Kissenger. The latter brought with it additional sensitivities and was, in some sense, enforcing a kind of intimacy that participants were more easily able to circumvent when producing their own prototypes. Likewise, we were conscious of needing to ensure each other's consent within the InTouch team when testing touch technologies with each other.

As part of *In Touch with Baby*, we had to navigate the already private and sensitive context of the home, as well as what was effectively medical and, thus, sensitive 'touch' data, in the form of babies' oxygen and heart rate readings. Not only was there a risk of revealing illicit touch in the home, it was important to ascertain and communicate to participants the details of what was happening to babies' data, how it was stored and who had access to it. In aggregate form, it was clear from our conversations with Owlet makers that there was also an aim to use OSS data to contribute to medical norms and definitions. Partly for health and safety reasons, it was important to know how accurate the OSS was in detecting babies' well-being and, further, how parents would make sense of touch data. The meanings parents came to attribute to the data – that is, of their child being healthy, a good sleeper – impacted on interaction and wider social relations (e.g. empathy, bonding). How touch becomes data is a question we continue to explore through our work, and an ethical question for both design and research on digital touch.

Throughout this chapter, we have outlined the ways in which touch might be digitally represented and reproduced, and we have hinted at what it might mean for these materialisations of touch to leave a digital trace. If wanting to infuse the design process with a sensitivity towards 'tactile data', it is useful to articulate how touch as data matters. There are, we argue, two hotspots of data use: first, as making sense of people's bodies (physiologically and emotionally) and, second, as learning about people's touch practices or behavioural patterns. The latter can be exploited for commercial gains (e.g. touch marketing); more generally, the tracking and analysis of behavioural touch data raises privacy and other ethical concerns when we return to questions of who decides on appropriate qualities or quantities of touch. Both of these hotspots are moreover linked to questions of touch as identifier, and of the trust we can place in the accuracy, completeness and representations of data.

7.6 Conclusion

In this chapter, we raised key questions of touch ethics and values in digitally mediated contexts. We outlined the tensions between universalistic notions of ethics, touch definitions and boundaries, and how these might be situationally complex. Specifically, we brought the complexities of 'the body' in its physiological, sociocultural and sensory manifestations to the forefront of digital touch, with a view to both exploring existing moments of digital touch interaction and designing new ones. Key sensitivities included the kinds of touches, movements, mobilities and socialities inscribed in touch interfaces and wider user experiences, and how we imagine and understand bodies, in terms of their agency, ability and diversity. Importantly, this chapter has moved some way beyond the intricacies of interaction design to also bring to the fore the wider social implications of digital touch, including questions of representation (of touch and bodies), touch norms and practices, and the nature and significance of tactile data. One way of embedding ethical values in the design of touch technologies is to attend to the sociotechnical imaginaries that guide our research and design, and the imaginations of those we design with and for (Chap. 6). More generally, we can think of the relationships and environments we create, that is, what kinds of relationships are enabled or restricted, whose rights are upheld, who is empowered, or not.

Just as we proposed following 'touch' in its different digital-material manifestations and its implications for bodies and social relationships, we also discussed key ethical concepts, such as consent, trust and control, as dynamic and multifaceted. The chapter highlights a tension between liberating and censoring digital touch, which we have not fully resolved. Instead, we suggest more research is needed to understand the social and psychological implications of emerging touch technologies, not just after the fact but also, crucially, at those opportune moments when early concepts, prototypes, user scenarios and wider discourses allow us to access social and sensory meanings and connotations of significance for future designs. This involves actively engaging with touch boundaries – not just as sets of rules but as talking points and sensitivities (Green 2016). Golmohammadi has written of her experiences of (unmediated) touch in a professional cuddle workshop (Golmohammadi 2019), which involved some ground rules – in this case, avoiding sexual contact but also asking for permission before touching. Thomas writes of generating a 'grammar' of touch and touch 'invitations' as part of establishing an 'ethics of care' in *Figuring*, a participatory virtual touch performance (Thomas 2018): 'it was essential to create ways in which participants would feel supported and cared for, but not bounded or contained in any way'. She took inspiration from contact improvisation, specifically work by Little (2014) which advocates the notion of 'response-ability' as a relational practice that responds and supports partners, rather than keep and restrain them.

Our research suggests that digital mediation has the potential to change sensations, communication practices and social and relations but that existing social boundaries still exist; they are felt and negotiated, both in the immediate interaction context and in wider meanings and connotation of mediated touch. Bringing the sensitivities and complexities of touch to the forefront of design – and making them a talking point in and through design – is one step towards safeguarding 'ethical touch'.

References

Arnold T, Scheutz M (2017) The tactile ethics of soft robotics: designing wisely for human–robot interaction. Soft Robot 4(2):81–87

Bardzell S, Bardzell J (2011) Towards a feminist HCI methodology: social science, feminism, and HCI. In: Proceedings of the SIGCHI conference on human factors in computing systems, CHI '11. ACM, New York, pp 675–684

Barzallo B, Punin C, Llumiguano C, Huerta M (2019) Wireless assistance system during episodes of freezing of gait by means superficial electrical stimulation. In: Lhotska L, Sukupova L, Lacković I, Ibbott GS (eds) World congress on medical physics and biomedical engineering 2018, IFMBE proceedings. Springer, Singapore, pp 865–870

Behrendt M (2018) Reflections on moral challenges posed by a therapeutic childlike Sexbot. In: 3rd international conference LSR 2017. Springer, London, pp 96–113

Benjamin R (2019) Race after technology: abolitionist tools for the new Jim Code, 1st edn. Polity, Medford

Blake RJC (2011) Ethnographies of touch and touching ethnographies: some prospects for touch in anthropological enquiries. Anthropol Matters 13:1

Bonde S, Briant C, Firenze P, Hanavan J, Huang A, Li M, Narayanan NC, Parthasarathy D, Zhao H (2016) Making choices: ethical decisions in a global context. Sci Eng Ethics 22(2):343–366

Botvinick M, Cohen J (1998) Rubber hands "feel" touch that eyes see. Nature 391:756

Caddy B (2019) Keeping virtual reality environments harassment-free. OneZero. https://onezero.medium.com/keeping-virtual-reality-environments-harassment-free-3b9d4e5d3416. Accessed 27 Apr 19

Classen C (2005) The book of touch. Berg Publishers, Oxford

Conte JR, Wolf S, Smith T (1989) What sexual offenders tell us about prevention strategies. Child Abuse Negl 13(2):293–301

Cranny-Francis A (2011) Semefulness: a social semiotics of touch. Soc Semiot 21(4):463–481

De Angeli A, Brahnam S, Wallis P, Dix A (2006) Misuse and abuse of interactive technologies. In: CHI '06 extended abstracts on human factors in computing systems, CHI EA '06. ACM, New York, pp 1647–1650

Devlin K (2018) Turned on: science, sex and robots. Bloomsbury Sigma, London

Dix A (2008) Response to "sometimes it's hard to be a robot: a call for action on the ethics of abusing artificial agents". Interact Comput 20(3):334–337

Drotner K (1999) Dangerous media? Panic discourses and dilemmas of modernity. Paedagog Hist 35(3):593–619

Elo M (2012) Digital finger: beyond phenomenological figures of touch. J Aesthet Cult 4(1):14982

Field T (2001) Touch. MIT Press, Cambridge, MA

Fogg BJ, Tseng H (1999) The elements of computer credibility, in: proceedings of the SIGCHI conference on human factors in computing systems, CHI '99. ACM, New York, pp 80–87

Frauenberger C, Rauhala M, Fitzpatrick G (2017) In-action ethics. Interact Comput 29(2):220–236

Friedman B, Kahn PH, Borning A (2008) Value sensitive design and information systems. In: The handbook of information and computer ethics. Wiley, Hoboken, pp 69–101

Golmohammadi L (2019) Cuddle workshops. -IN-TOUCH Digital Touch Communication. https://in-touch-digital.com/2019/05/28/cuddle-workshops/. Accessed 6.11.19

Green L (2016) The trouble with touch? New insights and observations on touch for social work and social care. Br J Soc Work 47(3):773–792

ISO (2009) Ergonomics of human-system interaction – Part 920: Guidance on tactile and haptic interactions. International Organization for Standardization, Geneva, Switzerland

Jacobs N, Huldtgren A (2018) Why value sensitive design needs ethical commitments. Ethics Inf Technol

Jewitt C, Leder Mackley K, Atkinson D, Price S (2020) Rapid prototyping for social science research. In: Pauwels L, Mannay D (eds) The SAGE handbook for visual research methods. Sage, London, pp 534–550

Kozel S (2007) Closer: performance, technology, phenomenology. MIT Press, Cambridge, MA

Leder Mackley K, Jewitt C, Price S (under review) In touch with baby: parenting and bio-sensing as mediated touch

Little N (2014) Restructuring the self-sensing: attention training in contact improvisation. J Dance Somat Pract 6(2):247–260

Lupton D, Williamson B (2017) The datafied child: the dataveillance of children and implications for their rights. New Media Soc 19(5):780–794

Muller M (2011) Feminism asks the "who" questions in HCI. Interact Comput 23(5):447–449

Munteanu C, Molyneaux H, Moncur W, Romero M, O'Donnell S, Vines J (2015) Situational ethics: re-thinking approaches to formal ethics requirements for human-computer interaction. In: Proceedings of the 33rd annual ACM conference on human factors in computing systems, CHI '15. ACM, New York, pp 105–114

O'Neill C (2017) Haptic media and the cultural techniques of touch: the sphygmograph, photoplethysmography and the apple watch. New Media Soc 19(10):1615–1631

Overgoor MLE, Kon M, Cohen-Kettenis PT, Strijbos SAM, de Boer N, de Jong TPVM (2006) Neurological bypass for sensory innervation of the penis in patients with spina bifida. J Urol 176(3):1086–1090

Parisi D (2008) Fingerbombing, or "touching is good": the cultural construction of technologized touch. Sens Soc 3(3):307–328

Parisi D (2018) Archaeologies of touch: interfacing with haptics from electricity to computing. University of Minnesota Press, Minneapolis

Price S, Leder Mackley K, Jewitt C, Huisman G, Petreca B, Berthouze N, Prattichizzo D, Hayward V (2018) Reshaping touch communication: an interdisciplinary research agenda. In: Extended abstracts of the 2018 CHI conference on human factors in computing systems, CHI EA '18. ACM, New York, pp W17:1–W17:8

Rheingold H (1991) Virtual reality: the revolutionary technology of computer-generated artificial worlds – and how it promises to transform society, reprinted edn. Simon & Schuster, New York

Richardson K (2016) The asymmetrical "relationship": parallels between prostitution and the development of sex robots. SIGCAS Comput Soc 45(3):290–293

Rode JA (2011) A theoretical agenda for feminist HCI. Interact Comput 23(5):393–400

Sadowski J (2014) Exoskeletons in a disabilities context: the need for social and ethical research. J Respons Innovat 1(2):214–219

Savvides L (2018) Wearing the Teslasuit is a shocking experience. CNET. https://www.cnet.com/news/wearing-the-teslasuit-is-a-shocking-experience/. Accessed 6.17.19

Sheila Media (2018) Creepy new "smart skin" making sex robots to FEEL human touch. Sheila Media. https://www.sheila.media/creepy-new-smart-skin-making-sex-robots-to-feel-human-touch-cyber-love-realistic-outperforms-human-skin/. Accessed 6.26.19

Sun X, Sugai F, Okada K, Inaba M (2018) Design and control of a novel robotic knee-ankle prosthesis system. In: 2018 7th IEEE international conference on Biomedical Robotics and Biomechatronics (Biorob). Presented at the 2018 7th IEEE international conference on Biomedical Robotics and Biomechatronics (Biorob), pp 737–743

Teh JKS, Cheok AD, Choi Y, Fernando CL, Peiris RL, Fernando ONN (2009) Huggy Pajama: a parent and child hugging communication system. In: Proceedings of the 8th international conference on interaction design and children, IDC '09. ACM, New York, pp 290–291

Thomas LM (2018). Figuring: bodies, materiality and touch in a multi-person virtual reality – developing an ethics of care/touch in participatory performance practice. IN-TOUCH Digital Touch Communication. https://in-touch-digital.com/2018/12/18/figuring-bodies-materiality-and-touch-in-a-multi-person-virtual-reality-developing-an-ethics-of-care-touch-in-participatory-performance-practice/. Accessed 6.11.19

van Erp JBF, Toet A (2013) How to touch humans: guidelines for social agents and robots that can touch. In: 2013 Humaine Association conference on affective computing and intelligent interaction. IEEE, pp 780–785

VWVR (2018) A vision for women and virtual reality. http://www.vwvr.org/. Accessed 6.27.19

Waycott J, Munteanu C, Davis H, Thieme A, Moncur W, McNaney R, Vines J, Branham S (2016) Ethical encounters in human-computer interaction. In: Proceedings of the 2016 CHI conference extended abstracts on human factors in computing systems, CHI EA '16. ACM, New York, pp 3387–3394

Whitby B (2008) Sometimes it's hard to be a robot: a call for action on the ethics of abusing artificial agents. Interact Comput 20(3):326–333

Winkler T, Spiekermann S (2018) Twenty years of value sensitive design: a review of methodological practices in VSD projects. Ethics Inf Technol:1388–1957

Chapter 8
Closing Thoughts, Insights and Resources for Digital Touch Communication Research and Design

Abstract This chapter closes the book with a note on thematic directions, in response to the speculative and emergent character of digital touch communication, signalling our desire and need to keep the conversation open. We point to the significance of a social take on digital touch, particularly with reference to the types of questions this perspective raises and the way it positions technology in relation to people and society more generally. We draw attention to the research insights on digital touch communication discussed throughout the book that may inform design. Finally, we comment on the theoretical and methodological routes that we have taken to research digital touch communication, and draw on the ideas and research presented in this book to sketch an emergent research and design framework for digital touch communication.

8.1 A Social Perspective on Digital Touch

The social take on digital touch provided in this book is significant for what gets brought into the scope of research and design, the types of questions raised, and the ways that technology is positioned as intrinsically linked to social relations, mutually shaping each other as they are developed and maintained.

Throughout the book, we have illustrated how developments in sensory digital technologies are bringing touch to the fore in ways that move digital communication beyond 'ways of seeing' to include new 'ways of feeling' and the competing discourses of desire and anxiety that this gives rise to. We have shown that this shift requires us to take new measure of digitally mediated touch, or 'digital touch', as a communicational resource. Through extensive engagement with the research literature and state-of-the-art digital touch devices, alongside a range of illustrative case study examples, we have explored what digital touch is (currently) and what it may come to be, how it is designed and imagined, and discussed people's imaginations of and responses to its communicative potentials and limitations. We examined how touch is conceptualized, imagined and experienced by people through different

C. Jewitt et al., *Interdisciplinary Insights for Digital Touch Communication*, Human–Computer Interaction Series,
https://doi.org/10.1007/978-3-030-24564-1_8

technologies and in different interactional contexts, the aspects of digital touch that are central to a range of communicational situations, how people improvise around digital touch and the skills, experiences and communicative repertoires that they draw on to do so. We have examined how designers and users take up the resources of touch that are available to them, and how the sensory-affective qualities and affordances, and the materiality of different touch technologies feature in different social and situated contexts. Through a social perspective, we have sought to understand how people take up and use digital touch technologies to mimic or supplement existing touch capacities and practices, heighten touch experiences, extend touch newly – for example, across distance, to be stored and shareable, or to reconfigure touch digitally to reshape what counts as touch and who and how we touch in various contexts. In doing so, the book documents key social resources for touch, the touch interactions supported and the kinds of touch communication practices that are being designed and identified, the social potentials and constraints of touch that are taken up by the designers of 'digital touch'. This extends to how digital touch technologies are situated and embedded in the wider contexts and experiences of everyday life, and how touch technologies require people to reimagine these for the future. Technological development in this area is still somewhat in its infancy and often remains at a 'proof of concept' stage; nonetheless, it is bringing a diverse set of techniques and engineering capacities, as well as various approaches to informing or underpinning designs and applications, depending on the area of use.

8.2 Insights for Digital Touch Communication

This book makes the case for a socially orientated and interdisciplinary approach to digital touch communication research and points to insights on key touch resources, dimensions and considerations that provide an emergent agenda for further digital touch communication research and design – starting routes or jumping off points, from which to further develop digital touch communication.

8.2.1 Social Norms and Digital Touch

Attending to the social norms that underpin people's touch interaction and communication, and how these are negotiated in social encounters, can provide a starting point from which to leverage understanding of the sociality of the tactile regime (Cranny-Francis 2011) in which they are embedded. Social norms of touch developed in relation to 'direct' touch, and its associated etiquettes and practices, have been (and will be) brought into the use and design of digital touch devices, systems and environments, albeit in uneven ways. Like digitally mediated visual communication, some norms and practices will be disrupted in 'translation', and it is likely that some new touch capacities and interactions will be elicited. In this fluid mix, unintended and unexpected consequences for how we communicate with others via touch will emerge. We suggest that this points to a need to consistently engage with the social and move beyond an emphasis on design explorations and point to solutions. Touch norms are significant in that they provide insights into the shared usage of touch for making culturally shared meaning of touch, and expectations of touch, which supports the imagination and design of digital touch communication. Understanding and reflecting on our own touch norms, as well as those of the people we research and/or design for, is therefore a useful route to recognising and benefiting from the potentials for difference and cultural flexibility towards new possibilities for designing digital touch communication. While on the one hand, understanding touch within the cultural complexities of the contemporary communicational landscape, characterised as it is by super-diversity, challenges the concept of social norms as stable and universal; on the other, gendered and cultural norms persist, perhaps more than ever given the hegemonic effect of the global circulation of technology. Given that social norms of touch are designed into and realised through the affordances of digital technologies, an awareness of the social norms of touch and how these regulate touch practices can help us to question, and/or engage newly with touch, from the mundane vibration of a phone in our pocket, to robotic-touch, and the innovation of contactless touch: the who, what, where, how and when of digital touch.

8.2.2 Touch Connections

The concepts of presence, absence and connection are significant technologically, socially, communicatively, sensorially, emotionally and imaginatively and, as such, central to the design and use of digital touch for communication. A social perspective on connection drives home the complexity of social presence and asserts that it goes well beyond being physically co-located. This opens up the design space and scope of what we might mean by producing 'presence' and 'connection' through digital touch, and suggests the need to attend to the situated social and sensorial meanings that emerge through interaction moments of which digital touch is a part. It also brings a number of tensions to the surface that can serve as important considerations for design, including the question of mimicking or replicating human touch versus touch at a symbolic or imagined level, which may give rise to new forms of sharing or experiencing through touch. Related to this is the tension between the significance of specific touch interfaces – their materiality, sensorial affordances, social connotations and functionality – and the idea that these might move into the background, or be personalised, and function as 'mere' mediators or enablers of digital touch communication. Throughout this book, we have argued that interfaces can be transformative or reductionist, depending on how advanced or situationally appropriate they 'feel'. Building on this, we suggest that they are strengthened by being sensitive to differently situated and experiencing bodies – shaped through the intersections of age, gender, different abilities, race and culture and personal preferences. We have also discussed how new touch technologies will emerge into an existing polymedia environment or technoscape, rather than existing in isolation, leading to notions of ambient touching and tactile presence with touch a part of the broader digital sensory terrain.

8.2.3 Sociotechnical Imaginaries of Digital Touch

This book has explored and made legible emerging sociotechnical imaginaries of digital touch to address how touch practices might be shaped through the uses of technology, and how this might in turn shape notions and practices of communication. We have fleshed out the sociality of digital touch communication by making legible emergent imaginaries of digital touch communication, providing critical understanding and insight on digital touch communication futures, and excavating and interrogating the features of sociotechnical imaginaries that 'tacitly' constrain and afford research and design of digital touch. We have discussed research participants' sociotechnical imaginaries of digital touch communication related to the body, temporality and spatiality, and drawn out three key themes that emerged through these articulations and deployments of the sociotechnical imaginary. These include speculations on touch with regard to the politics of touch, the representation of touch and the ethics of touch.

In addition to understanding the sociotechnical imaginaries that circulate among the users and contexts that we are researching and designing for, we make the case for exploring our own sociotechnical imaginaries, towards an explicit awareness of how they underpin and drive our research and design of digital touch. Such an awareness can, we argue, enable us to better articulate the social parameters that underpin our work, in order to understand how our imaginaries 'tacitly' constrain and afford research and design and provide a springboard from which to move beyond, extend, or disrupt them. The sociotechnical imagination enables us to glimpse some aspects of potential digital touch futures, and to engage with thinking what we want from the sociality of digital touch communication. Exploring sociotechnical imaginaries is therefore a vital resource towards a future methodology and agenda for the relatively uncharted territory of digital touch.

8.2.4 The Ethics of Touch

Across the book, we have raised key questions of touch ethics and values in digitally mediated contexts. We brought the complexities of 'the body' in its physiological, socio-cultural and sensory manifestations to the forefront of digital touch, with a view to both exploring existing moments of digital touch interaction and designing new ones. Key sensitivities included the kinds of touches, movements, mobilities and socialities inscribed in touch interfaces and wider user experiences, and how we imagine and understand bodies, in terms of their agency, ability and diversity. We argue that one way of embedding ethical values in the design of touch technologies is to attend to the sociotechnical imaginaries that guide our research and design, and the imaginations of those we design with and for, as well as the relationships and environments we create, that is, what kinds of relationships are enabled or restricted, whose rights are upheld, who is empowered, or not.

Just as we have proposed attending to touch in its different digital-material manifestations and its implications for bodies and social relationships, we have also discussed key ethical concepts, such as consent, trust and control, as dynamic and multifaceted. We highlighted a tension between liberating and censoring digital touch, which we have not fully resolved. Instead, we suggest more research is needed to understand the social and psychological implications of emerging touch technologies, not just after the fact but also, crucially, at those opportune moments when early concepts, prototypes, user scenarios and wider discourses allow us to access social and sensory meanings and connotations of significance for future designs. This involves actively engaging with touch boundaries – not just as sets of rules but as talking points and sensitivities. Our research suggests that digital mediation has the potential to change sensations, communication practices and social and relations but that existing social boundaries still exist; they are felt and negotiated, both in the immediate interaction context and in wider meanings and connotation of mediated touch. Bringing the sensitivities and complexities of touch to the forefront of design – and making them a talking point in and through design – is, we suggest, one step towards safeguarding ethical touch.

8.3 Methodologies for Digital Touch

In this book, we have discussed the many methodological challenges of researching digital touch communication at a time when technologies are evolving rapidly and are not yet 'domesticated', and methods and theories remain under-developed. Including the challenge of researching digital touch technologies that are unstable, lab-bound, researching digital touch with under-developed methods and theories; and the difficulty in observing, interpreting and making 'felt' touch experiences.

In response to these challenges, we have made the case for attending to the multimodal and multi-sensorial aspects of touch, making the sociality and sensorality of digital touch our starting point and focus. As such, we argue for an approach to digitally mediated touch as a communicative mode (a set of resources and principles for their organization and use), a sensorial experience entangled in the materiality and sociality of the body, the environment and technologies. Alongside this, we have maintained the significance of interdisciplinary dialogues for understanding touch, in particular with art, neuroscience, HCI and computer science, engineering, and design. In our broad theoretical framing, we have used a range of methods to engage participants in creative processes, making and bodily touchy-activities with themselves, others, materials and objects, and to deliberately go beyond the linguistic and the individual. These methods have included the development of design briefs, the design and use of technology-probes and artistic provocations, ethnographic encounters, in-depth interviews and focus groups centred around demonstrations with digital devices and environments, prototyping, speculative scenarios and role play with touch devices, and video re-enactments and walk-throughs (in the home, gallery, and virtual environments). In particular, we have illustrated the potential of prototyping to bridge interdisciplinary differences in the context of social science research collaborations with other disciplines, in order to gain access to and generate digital touch experiences and imaginations for research purposes. Collectively these methods provide opportunities for reflection on the rich complexities of touch and have proven to be particularly adept at accessing participants' sociotechnical imaginaries of digital touch communication. Generating new research spaces for digital touch can help to open up new routes for participants to reimagine touch and to explore the new social boundaries of digital touch communication. It has also enabled us to access participants' sociotechnical imaginaries of digital touch communication and to both explore and re-orientate to its past, present and futures.

8.4 An Emergent Research and Design Framework for Digital Touch Communication

Designing digital touch is complex, and we have set out to explore ways to prompt and support a broad, nuanced conception of digital touch. For example, drawing our research on digital touch communication into the development of a card-based resource, the Designing Digital Touch Toolkit, to support engagement with the complexities of working with touch across different stages of Design Thinking. We suggest that social science research can help to expand design processes through the emphasis that it puts on the social, sensory and communicative properties of touch to encourage greater awareness, discussion and investigation of digital touch. In this way, social science can raise questions to help designers reflect newly on their own and others' touch experiences; offer more conceptual or abstract prompts and provocation for thought or action; and suggest structured exercises to work through specific design elements for digital touch communication.

Building on the broad social, multimodal and sensorial foundation that underpins our work, and drawing on the ideas and research presented across the book chapters, we close this book by sketching an emergent framework to inform and support social, sensory and ethical research and design of digital touch communication (experiences, devices, systems and environments). This provisional Digital Touch Communication framework (Fig. 8.1) provides socially oriented frames of attention and an initial set of investigatory dimensions emerging out of the work discussed in this book with which to think through the social and sensorial

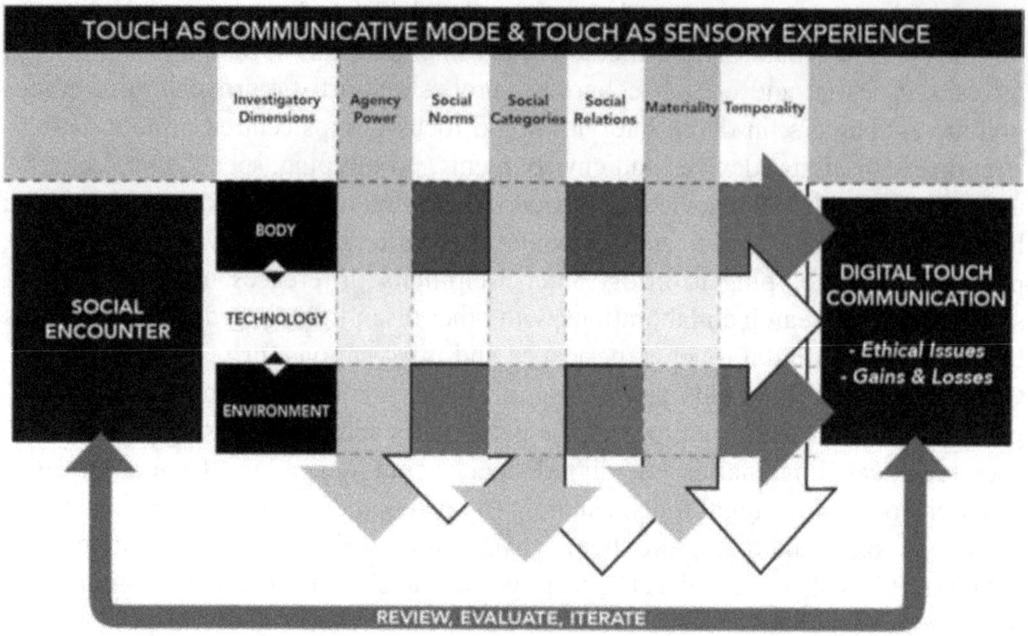

Fig. 8.1 Initial InTouch Research and Design Framework for Digital Touch Communication

components of digital touch communication. These are designed to support researchers and/or designers in the critical design and analysis of digital touch communication by attending to, and reflecting on, the ethical considerations raised, and the communicative gains and losses realised when touch is digitally mediated. At this early stage, the framework is tentative and intended as a springboard for future development and conceptualisation.

The over-arching 'frame of attention' that structures the framework, built on our theoretical stance, articulates a simultaneous concern with touch as a communicative mode and as sensorial experience. It requires, on the one hand, analytical attention towards the different modes and modal resources that are available within a given digital touch communication encounter (e.g. of movement, posture and gesture, gaze, visual representational modes, or sound – speech or music), and how these are taken up by users and orchestrated in relation to touch communication. On the other hand, and closely related to this multimodal attention, the frame also accounts for, and encourages reflection on, the ways in which touch is part of multisensorial experience and meaning-making.

This framing draws attention to a set of inter-related initial investigatory dimensions, which are realised through (and actualise) the social orchestration of modes and sensorial experience: agency and power – who or what touches; social norms of touch; social categories related to touch (e.g. gender) (as discussed in other chapters, such categories are continuously constructed and differently meaningful, rather than deterministic); social relations through touch; materialities of touch; and tactile temporalities. These dimensions will be refined and added to through the findings of future case studies and the analytical work of InTouch.

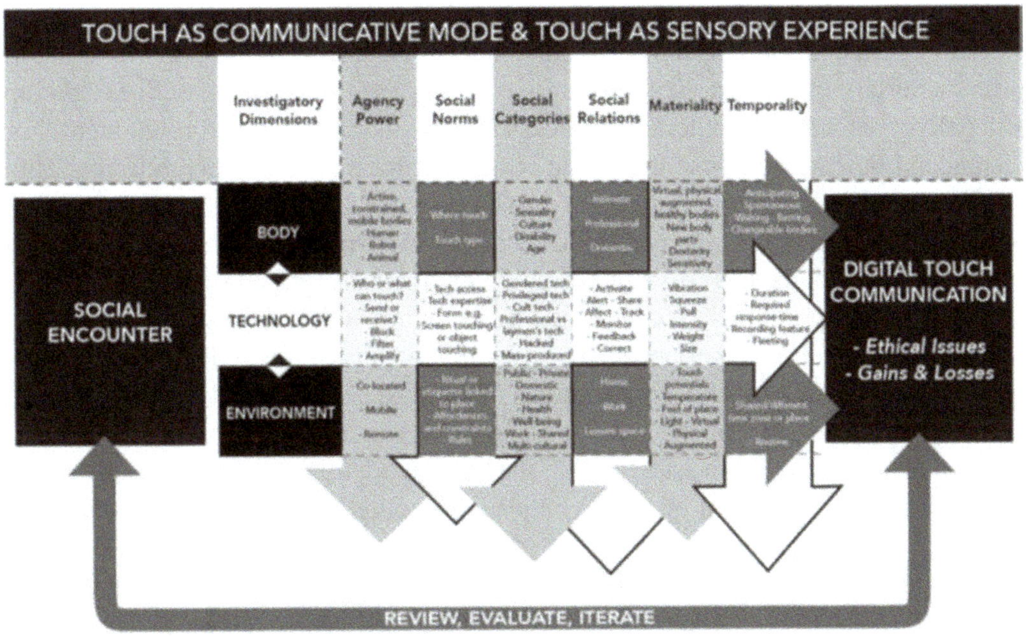

Fig. 8.2 An indication of the kinds of considerations and resources that might populate the Framework for Digital Touch Communication

We understand these social and sensorial dimensions of touch as being entangled in and produced through situated encounters (shaped by and shaping the social), in which the materiality and sociality of the body, the environment and technologies are key: these three interconnecting concepts (body, technology and environment) provide a second parallel set of investigatory considerations that structure the framework. While these three concepts are always in play and in interrelation, the framework can be used to bring them in and out of focus in order to emphasize specific aspects of digital touch within an encounter for the purposes of research and/or design.

A digital touch communication encounter may refer to the design process itself and a user may include designers and/or researchers. Touch communication and sensorial experiences are understood as a part of the production (and result of) social encounters - between humans, humans and objects, or humans and robots – in social, sensory and material environments. These encounters (e.g. medical, professional, or personal relationships) are shaped through (and shape) larger social framings imbued with particular and varying touch histories and practices.

We have populated the diagram of the Framework below (Fig. 8.2) to indicate the kinds of considerations and resources that might be interrogated in relation to its investigatory dimensions. These are intended as illustrative rather than exhaustive and serve to give a sense of the communicative and sensorial aspects of digital touch communication that can be brought into view through the framework. The Digital Touch Communication Framework can also be used alongside other research and design tools or frameworks (e.g. the Double Diamond Design Framework) (Design Council 2007).

The framework can be used in the process of designing a digital touch communication experience, or a specific digital touch device, system, or environment. It offers a variety of entry points into all design stages (i.e. discover, define, develop and deliver) as well as the iterative process of design evaluation and refinement. For instance, a designer can use the framework to bring a specific research or design consideration (e.g. Body and Agency) into focus, in relation to a specific user group and social encounter. They may use the framework to explore a particular dimension of touch, for instance they may interrogate how their design is or could utilise different tactile temporalities to consider the different impacts of these on their designed touch communication experience across the dimensions of the body, touch technology, and environment. The framework can be used to explore the design of a digital touch experience in a holistic way, looking across its dimensions by attending to how tweaks and changes in each 'cell' of the framework might shape that experience.

Similarly, in the context of researching digital touch communication, the framework provides a series of considerations to guide and frame attention. These may be used to generate interview or focus group questions, offer analytical dimensions in relation to specific digital touch communication devices as they feature in a particular social encounter, or provide a way to focus in on the body, technology, environment, temporality or other key aspects of the digital touch communication experience to sensitise the research to the multimodal, sensorial and social aspects of digital touch.

The thematic directions, emergent ideas, and provisional framework that this closing chapter, and the book more generally, offers highlights both the speculative and emergent character of digital touch communication and the value of bringing a social, multimodal and sensorial, perspective to the ongoing discussion of what people imagine and desire for digital touch communication, what it is and may come to be in our futures.

References

Cranny-Francis A (2011) Semefulness: a social semiotics of touch. Social Semiotics 21(4):463–481

Design Council (2007) Eleven lessons: managing design in eleven global companies. Design Council, London

www.ingramcontent.com/pod-product-compliance
Lightning Source LLC
LaVergne TN
LVHW082237200926
848484LV00008B/2367